IGNATIUS WAS GREEN

IGNATIUS WAS GREEN

Ecological Dimensions
OF THE *Spiritual Exercises*

MARGARET SCOTT, ACI

Paulist Press
New York / Mahwah, NJ

Scripture quotations are from *New Revised Standard Version Bible: Catholic Edition*, copyright © 1989, 1993 National Council of the Churches of Christ in the United States of America. Used by permission. All rights reserved worldwide.

Cover image by irin-k / Shutterstock.com
Cover and book design by Lynn Else

Copyright © 2025 by Margaret Scott, aci

All rights reserved. No part of this publication may be reproduced, stored in a retrieval system, or transmitted in any form or by any means, electronic, mechanical, photocopying, recording, scanning, or otherwise, without either the prior written permission of the Publisher, or authorization through payment of the appropriate per-copy fee to the Copyright Clearance Center, Inc., www.copyright.com. Requests to the Publisher for permission should be addressed to the Permissions Department, Paulist Press, permissions@paulistpress.com.

Library of Congress Cataloging-in-Publication Data
Names: Scott, Margaret, 1942- author.
Title: Ignatius was green: ecological dimensions of the spiritual exercises / Margaret Scott, aci.
Description: New York, Mahwah, NJ: Paulist Press, 2025. | Includes bibliographical references. | Summary: "This book traces St. Ignatius's love of nature underlying the text of the Spiritual Exercises"— Provided by publisher.
Identifiers: LCCN 2024010232 (print) | LCCN 2024010233 (ebook) | ISBN 9780809157167 (paperback) | ISBN 9780809188789 (ebook)
Subjects: LCSH: Ecology—Religious aspects—Catholic Church. | Ecotheology. | Ignatius, of Loyola, Saint, 1491–1556. | Spiritual exercises.
Classification: LCC BT695.5 .S337 2025 (print) | LCC BT695.5 (ebook) | DDC 261.8/8—dc23/eng/20240807
LC record available at https://lccn.loc.gov/2024010232
LC ebook record available at https://lccn.loc.gov/2024010233

ISBN 978-0-8091-5716-7 (paperback)
ISBN 978-0-8091-8878-9 (e-book)

Published by Paulist Press
997 Macarthur Boulevard
Mahwah, New Jersey 07430
www.paulistpress.com

Printed and bound in the
United States of America

I dedicate this book to the many Jesuits—confreres of Ignatius Loyola—who over the years, and in so many countries, have opened the treasures of the Spiritual Exercises *for me. It was an elderly Belgian Jesuit who encouraged me to join the congregation of the Handmaids of the Sacred Heart of Jesus precisely because of our Ignatian spirituality. Special thanks to Jesuit friends and colleagues, particularly in Saint Joseph's University, Philadelphia, and Comillas Pontifical University in Madrid, who have enabled me to discover hidden depths in the Exercises and accompany others on their Ignatian adventure. But above all, I owe a debt of gratitude to Jorge Bergoglio, SJ—better known as Pope Francis—who knows exactly how to weave this passion for creation seamlessly into his Ignatian identity.*

Contents

Introduction: Green Is Our Passion ix

1. Greening Christian Spirituality: Recapturing Care and Wonder 1
2. Ignatius's Roots; Ignatius's God: His Identity and World 17
3. Growing the Text of the *Spiritual Exercises:* From the Seeds of His Journey 27
4. God's Dream for Us: The Principle and Foundation 39
5. Creation Holds Its Breath: The First Week 48
6. The Creator Steps into Creation: The Second Week 56
7. Christ's Cross Is Every Tree: The Third Week 63
8. Very Early When the Sun Had Risen: The Fourth Week 69
9. Love Showered on All Creation: Contemplation to Gain Love 75
10. Conclusion: Green Was Ignatius's Passion 87

Notes 93

Selected Bibliography 105

Introduction

Green Is Our Passion

As St. Ignatius of Loyola limped slowly toward his personal sunset, he often gazed up at the Roman night sky, alive with hundreds of twinkling stars. A native son of the town of Azpeitia in Gipuzkoa, he had grown up nestled in the rural Basque countryside; but now he was trapped in an urban Italian landscape. Was he, perhaps, held lovingly by fond memories of Gipuzkoa's natural beauty? Its valleys and rivers, forests and paths, natural parks, and various kinds of eco-systems? Gipuzkoa, then and now, is lush and green, right to the sea, which turns bluish or gray depending on the sky, and has a mountainous and abrupt interior.

Gipuzkoa Turismoa describes the scenery of this small province this way: "Greenery is always in view and clearly stands out from all the other colors. It tinges the coasts, mountains, valleys, everything, accompanying the courses of rivers like inseparable friends. It is the tonality that distinguishes and unifies the province. Green is our passion."[1] Ignatius was born a true Gipuzkoan Basque. So, was Ignatius's passion green too?

Interestingly, there was a "green tinge" to Ignatius's post-cannonball convalescent reading. Always an avid reader, during this time of inactivity, Ignatius craved the romantic novels he was used to, but the only volumes available were the *Life*

IGNATIUS WAS GREEN

of Christ and the *Legenda Aurea*—the then immensely popular but lengthy encyclopaedic "lives of the saints." It is striking that Ignatius was touched above all by the lives of two of these saints: St. Francis of Assisi and St. Dominic. "What if I were to do what Saint Francis or Saint Dominic did?"[2] Of Francis, he read: "Francis, servant and friend of Almighty God, was born in the city of Assisi, and was made a merchant unto the twenty-fifth year of his age, and wasted his time by living vainly, whom our Lord corrected by the scourge of sickness, and suddenly changed him into another man."[3] Ignatius could identify with this beginning from his own story. The text continued describing how Francis, who found God in all creatures, identified with them as brother and sister:

> On a time he found a great multitude of birds, and then he said to them: My brethren, ye ought strongly to praise and give laud to your Maker which hath clad you with feathers and hath given to you pens for to fly and hath granted you the purity of the air and governed you without charge or business. And the birds turned their beaks or bills to him and spread their wings, and stretched their necks and addressed their heads and beheld him intently. And he passed forth by the middle of them so nigh that he touched them with his coat, and none of them arose out from his place till he gave to them leave that they flew together.
>
> On a time when he preached at the castle Almarye, and he might not be heard for the swallows which made their nests, to whom he said: My sister swallows, it is time that I speak, for ye have said enough, be ye now still till

Introduction

the word of God be accomplished. And they obeyed and were still anon.[4]

Did Francis's affinity with the natural world find an echo in Ignatius's heart? He would already have been familiar with the Franciscan order. There was even a Franciscan convent in Azpeitia, one of whose foundresses was a relative of his: María López de Emparán y Loyola.

As Ignatius's conversion evolved, we read in his autobiography of green touches at important moments in that process. During his time in Manresa, when God was dealing with him, "as a schoolteacher deals with a child, while instructing him,"[5] we note that he received a special grace. "One day it was granted to him to understand with great spiritual joy, the way in which God has created the world. He seemed to see a white object, with rays stemming from it, from which God made light."[6] Later, we read that on the bank of the Cardoner River, sparkling in the sunlight, where Ignatius sat praying:

> He sat down for a little while with his face to the river—Cardoner—which was running deep. While he was seated there, the eyes of his understanding began to be opened; though he did not see any vision, he understood and knew many things, both spiritual things and matters of faith and learning, and this was with so great an enlightenment that everything seemed new to him.[7]

It was as if he were a new man with a new worldview.

As the river flowed below him, God flooded Ignatius with an extraordinary light, a light "so bright that all these

IGNATIUS WAS GREEN

things seemed new to him,"[8] giving him a profound insight into the relationship of everything to God. A pivotal, life-changing experience on the bank of a river.

Many Ignatian scholars think that this vision was the basis for the Contemplation to Attain Love at the end of the *Spiritual Exercises*. In the Contemplation, we meet God, who is present in all things, who labors to transform creation, and who bathes all of creation in a ceaseless flow of blessings and gifts, like the light emanating from the sun.

Was Ignatius passionate about being green? We don't know. But what we do know is that there are ecological insights contained in the content and dynamic of the *Spiritual Exercises* that speak of an author who was close to and in contact with the natural world and who was on intimately familiar terms with God, the Creator of that world. These insights have imbued Ignatian spirituality and marked the Society and its members over the years, including Jorge Bergoglio, SJ, who, in many ways "is doing what St. Francis did."[9] These insights have found their latest expression in the Fourth Universal Apostolic Preference of the Society: "Caring for our Common Home: Collaborate, with Gospel depth, for the protection and renewal of God's Creation."

1

GREENING CHRISTIAN SPIRITUALITY

Recapturing Care and Wonder

The little yellow flowers that nobody notices are saints looking up into the face of God.

—Thomas Merton

The climate crisis forces us to unearth a spirituality that is green, delightfully green. As Ellen Bernstein opines:

> I have long thought that the climate crisis was a spiritual crisis, a crisis in how we think about the world and what we value. It's a reflection of a fundamental breakdown in the way we treat each other and the Earth. Our religious traditions must take responsibility for helping us navigate the troubled waters we are facing. When we dig more deeply into our religious roots, we find ancient wisdom that can draw us closer to God's green Earth, cultivate in us a generosity toward all beings and steer us on paths of justice and

IGNATIUS WAS GREEN

righteousness that will ensure a healthy future for the Earth and all of us.[1]

Sandra Schneiders defines spirituality as "the actualization of the basic human capacity for transcendence."[2] For her, spirituality is not a series of practices, pious or otherwise, and it is certainly not a doctrine. Rather, it denotes a lived experience—a conscious involvement. Schneiders develops her definition by attributing four characteristics to spirituality: it is an ongoing project for a way of living; its ultimate purpose is integration; it is a process of self-transformation; and it is oriented toward the "ultimate good, the highest value." Christian spirituality, she adds, specifically identifies "the horizon of the ultimate value or good as the triune God revealed in Jesus Christ."[3] In other words, Christian spirituality is a relationship with the God who is "Lover, Beloved and Love."[4] It is being loved, passionately and tenderly, by that God, and loving that God with our whole being. It is a relationship that defines who we are and what we do. It focuses our vision to see that God is everywhere, in all things—in other people, communities, movements, events, places, the environment, the world at large, and the cosmos.

At the same time, Christian spirituality is lived out in the real world—in the concrete details of daily life, permeating the life of the Church at every level. It reaches out rather than looks inward in a self-referential focus on personal sanctification. It does so quietly and reverently. Christian spirituality walks hand in hand with public theology to the peripheries where God walks lovingly among real people with faces and names, described so powerfully by Gerard Manley Hopkins:

Greening Christian Spirituality

> For Christ plays in ten thousand places,
> Lovely in limbs, and lovely in eyes not his
> To the Father through the features of men's
>   faces.[5]

A spirituality centered on the person of Christ, "the firstborn of all creation" (Col 1:15) embraces our global reality, with all the issues generated by the rapidly changing world landscape with its environmental, economic, geopolitical, and cultural upheavals. It nurtures communion with the God who holds us in existence and cherishes all the creatures in our common home, and who is present in every human venue and activity, for there is no corner of human affairs where God is not alive and active. In this context, the current environmental crisis that is threatening the planet and the debate surrounding it forces us, as men and women of prayer, to renew our understanding of Christian spirituality and our relationship with God and God's creation. To revisit the ecological dimension of who we are and what we do, of our identity and our mission in the Church and the world. And, as we gently nurture the fragility of the environment, we discover the ecological dimensions of a spirituality that respects both the soul and the soil. In the words of Pope Francis: "The entire material universe speaks of God's love, his boundless affection for us. Soil, water, mountains: everything is, as it were, a caress of God."[6]

If we unpack the global context of our spirituality, we discover a world stumbling to the brink of ecological collapse and, despite the doubts of a few skeptics, glimpsing with dread the nearing "tipping point" of irreversible climate change. The disruption of the earth's climate has already begun to seriously influence the global economy

IGNATIUS WAS GREEN

and international relations in our rapidly warming world. We receive almost daily updates on social media about the worsening climate crisis. A few examples suffice: "Off the chart temperatures. Ocean surface heat skyrocketed over the course of several weeks. Scientists are alarmed"; "More than 13,000 people in Western Canada evacuated as wildfires rage across the region"; "This area of Spain (Seville) could be too hot for tourists"; "East African drought would not have happened but for humans, news science says"; "Monster heatwaves, snowpacks and floods: world extreme weather events are warnings of what's to come"; "At least 129 dead due to torrential rainfall in Rwanda"; "Meanwhile, in central California, fears are growing over flooding following extreme conditions which saw record levels of 'snowpack' and rain"; and "Climate change is causing 'trouble in paradise' for Pacific Island Nations."[7]

At the same time, with the increasing catastrophic impacts of climate change and the staggering loss of biodiversity, support for combating climate change has been growing. It is on the agenda of international gatherings. Some governments are, at last, investing in green recovery to create jobs and cut emissions, for carbon-free energy is now within reach. More companies are making bigger sustainability commitments in shorter time frames and promoting responsible climate choices in the face of heightened concerns by investors. In April 2023, the *National Catholic Reporter* carried a story about those concerns: "More than 31% of Citigroup shareholders supported a resolution brought by Catholic congregations that called for a review of the global bank's financing policies around climate change and Indigenous rights after Citigroup pumped billions of dollars into oil pipeline companies in recent years."[8] As faith groups throughout the world have stopped investing in coal, oil, and gas, "de-investment" has become the new buzzword. Young people are especially concerned about the effects of climate change on their future. In the preface to the Italian book *The Taste for Change: Ecological Transition as the Path to Happiness*[9] that looks at the connection between global economics and environmental destruction, Pope Francis writes: "We must admit with sincerity that it is the young people who embody the change we all objectively need." He continues to note that young people are asking older people "to change. Change our lifestyle, so predatory toward the environment. Change our relationship with the Earth's resources, which are not infinite. Change our attitude toward them, the new generations, from whom we are stealing the future."[10]

These young people have been stirred to action led by young women and men like Leah Namugerwa, from Uganda, who plants trees; Anuna De Wever, the Belgian teenager who was one of the first to organize a school strike to support the climate movement; Jerome Foster II, the youngest-ever White House advisor; Haven Coleman, cofounder of the American U.S. Youth Climate Strike; and of course, Greta Thunberg, the young Swedish activist.

More and more documentaries and books are being published that explain the science clearly. Among them is *The Climate Book* that was published in May 2023 by the same Greta Thunberg. This amazing young woman convened one hundred global scientists to explain in ordinary language and with simple graphics the climate crisis that is threatening our planet, while offering glimpses of the hope that it is still possible to avert a total climate meltdown, if we act now.

Global coalitions and movements to combat climate change are multiplying at national and international levels.

IGNATIUS WAS GREEN

Big "names" are now associated with the issue, such as Al Gore, David Attenborough, and so on. Celebrities, too, are joining the cause, including Harrison Ford, Leonardo DiCaprio, Shailene Woodley, Meryl Streep, Jane Fonda, Don Cheadle, and Ben Affleck, to name but a few. Prince William and his father, King Charles III, have also joined the cause.

The United Nations has also been intensifying pressure on international leaders. In 2015, the landmark UN Climate Change Conference, COP 21, drew up the Paris Agreement—a legally binding international agreement on climate change, adopted by 196 countries. Its goal was to limit global warming at well below 2, preferably 1.5 degrees, Celsius. Six years later, on August 9, 2021, the Intergovernmental Panel on Climate Change (IPCC) Report announced, "a code red for humanity," given that "the world is dangerously close to irreversible global warming unequivocally caused by human activities." This report was followed by two crucial UN conferences: The UN Biodiversity Conference on October 11–24, 2021, in Kunming, China, and the UN Climate Change Conference (COP 26) held on November 1–12, 2021, in Glasgow, Scotland.

However, COP 26 came and went leaving behind a disappointing legacy. Retired Bishop Erwin Kräutler of Xingú, Brazil, analyzed the outcome in medical terms: "Our planet is in intensive care, but COP 26 delayed treatment." COP 27 followed in 2022 and was also greeted with disappointment. Once again, definitive conclusions were elusive and failed to yield commitments to make substantive progress toward the three goals of the Paris Agreement. There was one breakthrough moment toward the end of COP 27, namely, the creation, finally, of a "loss and damage fund" for countries most impacted by climate change. However, that too was muted by the omission in the final text for a call and timeline to phase out all fossil fuels, while the promised funding remains a mere trickle relative to the trillions of dollars needed.

LAUDATO SI'

It was Pope Francis who anticipated the Paris Agreement in 2015, with his "green encyclical," *Laudato si'*, which built on and took to unimaginable heights the "green stance" already taken by his predecessor, Pope Benedict XVI. *Laudato si'* provides a spiritual perspective to the environmental debate with its systematic overview of the crisis from a religious and spiritual perspective. Until then, the environmental dialogue had been framed mainly in political, scientific, and economic terms. With this new encyclical, the language of faith entered the discussion—clearly and decisively. The encyclical firmly grounds the debate in a spiritual context and invites others to listen to a religious point of view, particularly its understanding of creation as a holy and precious gift from God to be reverenced by all men and women, and offering "ample motivation" to Christians and other believers "to care for our common home."[11] *Laudato si'* was truly a groundbreaking document that expanded the conversation by inviting dialogue and providing fresh insights.[12]

Eight years later, on October 4, 2023, Pope Francis also anticipated COP 28 that was scheduled to be held in Dubai that same year, by publishing the apostolic exhortation entitled *Laudate Deum*, which integrates science and theology. Here, the pope laments that our responses to the challenge to combat the climate crisis over the last thirty years have been inadequate and issues a call to action:

IGNATIUS WAS GREEN

> To say there is nothing to hope for would be suicidal, for it would mean exposing humanity, especially the poorest to the worst impacts of climate change...we can keep hoping that COP28 will allow for a decisive acceleration of energy transition, with effective commitments subject to ongoing monitoring....Once and for all let us put an end to the irresponsible derision that would present this issue as something merely ecological, "green," romantic frequently subject to ridicule by economic interests.[13]

The pope also reiterates the spiritual dimension that underpins the "pilgrimage of reconciliation with the world that is our home and to help make it more beautiful, because that commitment has to do with our personal dignity and highest values" (LD 69). For Francis, care for our common home is a journey of *communion* and *commitment*.

But this spiritual dimension resides within a biblical framework that encompasses the whole of God's Word, from the first pages that tell the story of creation:

> In the beginning when God created the heavens and the earth, the earth was a formless void and darkness covered the face of the deep, while a wind from God swept over the face of the waters....God saw everything that he had made, and indeed, it was very good. (Gen 1:1–2, 31)

The same theme is found in the psalms that marvel at God's majesty in creation:

Greening Christian Spirituality

> O Lord, our Sovereign, how majestic is your name in all the earth!...When I look at your heavens, the work of your fingers, the moon and the stars that you have established... (Ps 8:1, 3)[14]

Furthermore, in *Laudato si'*, Pope Francis notes:

> Jesus was able to invite others to be attentive to the beauty that there is in the world because he himself was in constant touch with nature, lending it an attention full if fondness and wonder. As he made his way throughout the land, he often stopped to contemplate the beauty sown by his Father and invited his disciples to perceive a divine message in things. (no. 97)

Indeed, nature played an important role in Jesus's life. He spent forty days in the desert "with the wild beasts," he prayed on mountaintops, often preached on the shores of the Sea of Galilee, and rode into Jerusalem on a donkey. Many of his parables are centered on nature. For example, when he spoke about God and God's kingdom, he uses the imagery of seeds and vines, birds of the air, sheep, trees, lilies of the field, and even foxes. Jesus, the Lord of Creation, calms the storm, walks on the waves, and identifies with the natural elements of water, light, bread, and wine. We know from John's Gospel that God loves creation so very much:

> For God so loved the *world* that he gave his only Son, so that everyone who believes in him may not perish but may have eternal life. Indeed, God did not send the Son into the *world* to condemn

IGNATIUS WAS GREEN

the *world*, but in order that the *world* might be saved through him. (John 3:16–17)

In Greek, the text reads: "God so loved the cosmos." This original reading invites us to contemplate the cosmos cherished gently and fondly by God and, at the same time, it challenges us to love and sustain the earth too. The same theme of creation is found in St. Paul's letter to the Colossians: "For in him [Jesus Christ] all things in heaven and on earth were created, things visible and invisible…the gospel that you heard, which has been proclaimed to every creature under heaven" (Col 1:16, 23). Finally, the theme of creation reaches its climax in the "new heaven and the new earth" foretold at the end of the Apocalypse (cf. Rev 21:1).

The "green" or ecological dimension of Christian spirituality has always existed. It is a dimension that has its basis in the writings of the early Fathers of the Church. Basil of Caesarea (330–379), founder of Eastern monasticism, called on all Christians to meditate on blades of grass and specks of dust because reflecting on the "beauty and grandeur" of creation—"earth, air, sky, water, day, night, all visible things"—is "training ground" for the soul to "learn to know God, since by the sight of visible and sensible things our intellect is led, as by a hand, to the contemplation of invisible things."[15] St. Augustine of Hippo (354–430) called on his readers to "observe the beauty of the world, and praise the plan of the creator. Observe what he made, love the one who made it. Hold on to this maxim above all; love the one who made it, because he also made you, his lover, in his own image."[16]

The ecological dimension emerges again in the early Middle Ages, after the encounter between Christianity and the Celtic tradition's intimate relationship with the environment that generated a holistic and integrated Christian spirituality.

The medieval figure best known for his love of nature is undoubtedly Francis of Assisi. His famous "Canticle of the Creatures" has long been considered a love letter to God's creation. For Francis, nature showed the footprints of where God had passed. Flowers reflected his beauty, the sun was a shadow of his brightness, the mountains were the strength of his arm. The sunrise reminded him of the rising of Christ. The song of a bird, the scurry of a squirrel, the babbling of brook, were all signs pointing to the presence and provident love of God. Nature lifted its unthinking prayer to God just through being what it was—God's creation.

Outstanding also is the delicately feminine environmental awareness evident in the music and writings of Hildegard of Bingen, the twelfth-century German Benedictine abbess, whose verdant inspiration was nurtured by the "greening power" of the beautiful Rhineland landscapes and the the forests around the monasteries in which she resided. "In the beginning all creatures were green and vital. They flourished amidst flowers," so writes Hildegard of Bingen in her praise of the divine greening power, the *viriditas* of God.[17] "O most honored Greening Force, You who roots in the Sun; You who lights up, in shining serenity, within a wheel that earthly excellence fails to comprehend. You are enfolded in the weaving of divine mysteries."[18] Reflecting on God's creative activity, Hildegard even hears God speak: "With my mouth, I kiss my own chosen creation. I uniquely, lovingly embrace every image I have made out of earth's clay."[19]

This "greening" of Christian spirituality extends beyond those older traditions to other spiritual writers.

IGNATIUS WAS GREEN

One example is St. Ignatius of Loyola, founder of the Society of Jesus and author of many documents,[20] including the *Spiritual Exercises*, which is a classic in Catholic spirituality and the source of Ignatian spirituality. A re-reading of *The Spiritual Exercises of St. Ignatius* reveals their ecological insights—from the "Principle and Foundation" to the "Contemplation to Obtain Love"—enriching our contemplative experience of creation, offering conversion, healing our relationships with God and all created things, and calling us to action for the sake of the earth. At a time of ecological crisis, his spiritual wisdom and mysticism offer new insights to address environmental concerns and a relevant contribution to the current ecological debate. Indeed, Fr. Arturo Sosa, SJ, the current General of the Society of Jesus, claims that "care for our common home is anchored in Ignatian spirituality."[21]

The imagery of many other classical spiritual authors and mystics reveals a similar ecological consciousness as an inherent part of their spirituality. But with the passing of time, that awareness became dulled and the memory of it forgotten. It is only recently, as we move into the emerging era of "cosmic consciousness," that there is a shift in our understanding of spirituality, especially Christian spirituality, to embrace more explicitly its ecological dimension, drawing our attention to the cosmos as a place of God's self-revelation and demanding that our relationship to God be developed in the context of our relationships with the cosmos in its totality. "We adore God," writes Douglas Burton-Christie, "woven into the very fabric of the universe, into every living being, every place, every person."[22] Or as Thomas Merton writes in his well-known interpretation of Exodus 3:5: "For the place where you stand is holy ground":

Greening Christian Spirituality

The pale flowers of the dogwood outside this window are saints. The little yellow flowers that nobody notices on the edge of that road are saints looking up into the face of God.

This leaf has its own texture and its own pattern of veins and its own holy shape, and the bass and trout hiding in the deep pools of the river are canonized by their beauty and their strength.

The lakes hidden among the hills are saints, and the sea too is a saint who praises God without interruption in her majestic dance.

The great, gashed, half-naked mountain is another of God's saints. There is no other like him. He is alone in his own character; nothing else in the world ever did or ever will imitate God in quite the same way.[23]

Later, Thomas Berry, a Passionist priest and one of the leading voices in "ecospirituality," opined: "There is now a single issue before us: survival. Not merely physical survival, but survival in a world of fulfilment, survival in a living world, where the violets bloom in the springtime, where the stars shine down in all their mystery, survival in a world of meaning."[24] Berry suggested that there is a spiritual dimension to our present ecological crisis. It has long been understood by Indigenous peoples that our relationship to the Earth is spiritually as well as physically sustaining. For Indigenous peoples, this is often included in their way of life and expressed through their rituals and prayers.

When I was living in Chile, I experienced how the Mapuche people receive their energy and wellbeing from the earth, the trees, and the snow-covered "Cordillera"

IGNATIUS WAS GREEN

mountains. I have watched while they listen attentively, their ears pressed to the ground—to "our mother's" heartbeat—as they connect with her rhythm in a symphony of beating hearts.

Today, we are witnessing an indigenization of Christian ecological spiritualty with the growing awareness of the cosmologies of Indigenous peoples and the writings of Indigenous scholars. H. Daniel Zacharias, from Treaty One Territory in Canada, writes: "For a long time, Western Christians have been taught that the land belongs to humans. The Bible teaches that humans belong to the land."[25] While Robin Wall Kimmerer goes as far as to state that Earth is a spiritual mother that humans depend on for life. Kimmerer draws on both Western science and Indigenous wisdom to form a unitive vision of all creation, with humanity a small yet important part. Plants are living beings with whom our proper relationship is kinship. Like other relatives, we have reciprocal responsibilities and must dialogue with them.

The ecological dimension of Christian spirituality is woven into a rich theological tapestry with its intertwining strands of traditional doctrine and newer insights. Our experience of wonder when engaging with creation echoes the sacramental imagination of Catholicism, in which the material world is understood as gift that points us to the Creator-who-became-flesh, who became a creature like us: "The Body of Christ. Amen."

In this context, *The Spiritual Exercises of St. Ignatius* have been a powerful instrument in shaping Christian life and spirituality for four centuries. They have inspired and energized countless people—Jesuits, other religious men and women, laymen and women of all Christian traditions, and many others. But how do they contribute to the spirituality of Christians today who inhabit a highly complex and interdependent world with its rapidly changing scientific, economic, diplomatic, political, ethical and, above all, ecological concerns? How do the writings of Ignatius contribute to the current ecospirituality debate?

Obviously, our world is very different today from what it was when Ignatius wrote the *Exercises*. His worldview was based on a feudal culture and an anthropocentric understanding that objectified the natural world, reducing its elegance and innate creativity to something to be conquered and controlled, true to the spirit of the Spanish *conquistadores*.

The insights of modern science, especially quantum physics, have engendered an awareness of the interconnectedness of all things and all people. We are told that the physical world is an inseparable whole, that every particle of creation is interconnected with every other particle, a cosmic identity. Furthermore, we live in a complex and highly interwoven, globalized world—technologically, socially, and culturally. Our spirituality is increasingly holistic and environmental and our theology more and more evolutionary. It is surprising, therefore, to discover that in the *Exercises*, Ignatius steps out of the limited, dualistic perspective of the sixteenth century, to introduce the twenty-first–century retreatant, into an integrated spiritual experience. The *Exercises* plunge the retreatant into a cosmic world, wrapped in the wonder of God, "Our Creator and Lord,"[26] who is actively at work through the length and breadth of all reality. This Ignatian ecological intuition is present throughout the *Exercises*.

So let us now allow Ignatius to lead us to seek and to find the mystery of God in the heart of all created things. For the *Exercises*, from beginning to end, are about an

IGNATIUS WAS GREEN

encounter with God, "Our Creator and Lord." I have used the translation of the *Spiritual Exercises* by Eric Jensen, SJ, called *The Spiritual Exercises of Saint Ignatius Loyola: Study Edition*.[27] It is a reader-friendly version and based on the Vulgate and the *Autograph* texts. Even though the *Autograph* was penned by a copyist, St. Ignatius personally corrected the sixteenth-century text and made additions to it in his own hand, and scholars tend to consider this text the most authentic. But, to appreciate the Ignatian text more fully, it is important to read it in the late medieval and early Renaissance context in which St. Ignatius lived, and against the background of the events and theology that shaped his spiritual experience, together with his personal, cultural, and religious roots.

2

IGNATIUS'S ROOTS; IGNATIUS'S GOD

His Identity and World

Ignatius was brought up in the lap of nature.

—Hedwig Lewis, SJ

Ignatius of Loyola's roots can be traced back to Spain. He was born in 1491. His birthplace was the castle of Loyola in Azpeitia, in the Basque province of Gipuzkoa in northern Spain. He was born into the medieval world of a family of minor Basque aristocrats. Both his father and his mother, who died when Iñigo was still young, were of an ancient and illustrious lineage. Theirs was a noble family steeped in chivalry, and loyal service and defense of the king.[1] They were a traditional Catholic family and the Catholic faith would have also been part of Ignatius's heritage. It flowed through his veins; it was part of his DNA. Although sincere, that faith would have had little to do with Church teaching or everyday life, and a great deal to do with family tradition, honor, pious practices, and patron saints.[2] As Margaret Silf aptly states: "High beliefs but low standards you might say. Brawls-on-Saturdays and Mass-on-Sundays, kind of thing."[3] When baby Iñigo opened his eyes, he would have seen a Spain that had burst onto the world stage as the most powerful country in Europe and the protagonist of Catholicism, international trade, and the arts.

SIXTEENTH-CENTURY SPAIN

In Rome, a Spanish pope had been elected while, at home, Spain was united under the Catholic King Ferdinand and Queen Isabella, who after defeating the Moors in Granada, ruled most of Spain. The large numbers of Moors and Jews in Spain had been given the ultimatum: convert to Christianity or face exile or death. In the sixteenth century, Catholicism was a strong bond that held Spaniards together. During that period, the Catholic Church was influenced by the historical, social, and cultural events of the time both in its spirituality and religious expressions—Bible-based and Christ-centered but militant in the wake of the "reconquest" with a powerful desire to convert new Christians, and fired by its burgeoning colonization. It was a militant Catholicism, marked by a spirit of action and the power of the cross.

The Inquisition, perhaps the most controversial act of Ferdinand and Isabella, was established in Castille in 1478, to investigate the suspicion of heresy among the Jewish *conversos* ("converts"). But its function overlapped both political and religious spheres, and its impact on Spanish society was felt for centuries. At the same time, numerous religious communities had sprung up, including monasteries of contemplatives, such as Cistercians and Carthusians. Medieval devotions included the cross and passion of Christ, Mary the Mother of Christ, and the cult of the

Ignatius's Roots; Ignatius's God

saints. Marian devotion was very much part of the religious environment that Ignatius was born into and grew up in, because it was very much part of Basque and Spanish religiosity. This is abundantly clear in Ignatius's *Autobiography*, notably in his choice of the Marian monastery of Montserrat as the key place in his conversion narrative and the bizarre incident with the Muslim, who did not believe in the virginity of Mary, and whom Ignatius's devotion and knightly training urged him to kill for such a perceived insult. Also, in the *Spiritual Exercises*, he suggests frequent colloquies with Our Lady, asking her to place him with her son.

Iñigo also lived in an era populated by famous explorers and adventurers. He would have been only one year old when, according to the popular rhyme, "in 1492 Columbus sailed the ocean blue" and discovered the New World. Spain, together with Portugal, explored the world's seas and opened new international sea routes. With the conquest of the New World, exploration ripened into colonization, and large parts of those territories became Spanish colonies, with the resulting new responsibility of administering these conquered lands, populated by unknown peoples, who had to be governed and assimilated. Tremendous violence imposed a society structured by domination at all levels through the superiority of elite Western European culture. Catholic missionary priests and religious accompanied the *conquistadores* with the blessing of a Church bent on converting the conquered peoples to Christianity. Later, Bartolome de las Casas, the Dominican missionary to the Native Americans, would become the first social voice raised to protect what he deemed the smallest and most forgotten of God's people. The Spanish also opened trade routes across the Pacific Ocean, linking the Americas with

IGNATIUS WAS GREEN

Asia. New and immeasurable riches came flowing into Spain's many ports, contributing to the rising power of the towns. However, this newfound wealth did not "trickle down" and extreme poverty was widespread.

It was also a time of famous European writers, artists, and scientists, like Michelangelo, El Greco, Raphael, Cervantes, and Palestrina, who inspired a rebirth in learning that expanded the boundaries of culture: the Renaissance and its rampant anthropocentrism.

Ignatius also lived during a period of contrasts and paradoxes, of controversy, of Reformation and Counter-Reformation. The sixteenth century also witnessed a shift from a late-medieval worldview to the dawn of the "Spanish Golden Age." Hence, at the beginning of the sixteenth century, there was a growing sense of pride and self-confidence. This pride extended to other fields: universities were founded reflecting the new humanism imported from Italy. Artists from around Europe, particularly from Flanders and Italy, traveled to the Iberian Peninsula to seek favor at the Spanish court, and artworks flowed in from various parts of Europe. Paintings and tapestries were eagerly bought by wealthy Spanish collectors, including the Queen. Thus it was that young Iñigo's roots were planted and grew deep down into the soil of a country full of self-confidence, excitement, and cruelty.

THE YOUNG IÑIGO

Iñigo, the youngest of thirteen children, was an ambitious young man who had no desire to stay at home with his older brothers, who had already won honor and wealth. He wanted to become a courtier. So, as a teenager, he was sent to Arevalo to serve as a page to a maternal relative,

Ignatius's Roots; Ignatius's God

Don Juan Velázquez de Cuellar, the treasurer of the kingdom of Castile. There, he learned what any young gentleman of his time needed to know: how to be a good soldier, an accomplished horseman, and courtier. There was a well-stocked library in Arevalo which allowed the young Iñigo to pursue his love of reading. He also learned to improve his handwriting and was considered a good writer. He would also have learned the virtues of discipline and obedience.

In 1517, he entered the service of another kinsman, the Duke of Nájera, viceroy of the northern part of the kingdom of Navarre, which bordered with France. For eleven years, Ignatius learned skills of administration, diplomacy, arms, and courtly manners. But his new life also featured dueling, gambling, dancing, and romancing with young ladies at court. He became involved in brawls, one of which resulted in charges being filed against him. In his autobiography, Ignatius refers to this period in his life: "Up to his twenty-sixth year the heart of Ignatius was enthralled by the vanities of the world. His special delight was in the military life, and he seemed led by a strong and empty desire of gaining for himself a great name."[4]

Ignatius was, in fact, a courtier, but in May 1521, he found himself defending the fortress of Pamplona against the French as a military officer. This second career came to an abrupt halt when a French cannonball badly injured both his legs. During his convalescence on the third floor of the family castle at Loyola, Ignatius experienced a profound conversion. A new desire to serve Christ the King replaced his former dreams of glory. His first efforts in this new service led to a complete reversal of values from someone given over to the "vanities of the world" to a total commitment to Christ.

IGNATIUS WAS GREEN

CONVERSION AND TRANSFORMATION

During his recuperation, Ignatius asked for romances "to pass away the time," but the only books available were *The Life of Christ*, by Ludolph of Saxony, and another book called the *Flowers of the Saints*, both in Spanish.[5] These readings attracted and transformed him. At the same time, Ignatius began to take notes of his reactions, thoughts, and spiritual insights, in a specially prepared book of "polished and lined paper...which he carried around very carefully."[6] On reflection, Ignatius became aware of different spirits stirring within him during and after his reading and also after his daydreams of winning the love of a noble lady. This experience provided the initial inspirational underpinning for the later *Spiritual Exercises* and, in particular, the rules for the Discernment of Spirits.

Once recovered, Ignatius set out for Jerusalem. One of his first stops on the way was at the shrine of Our Lady at Montserrat where he left his sword and donned pilgrim attire. From there he went to Manresa where he underwent intense spiritual growth. That growth was, Ignatius recalls in his autobiography, nurtured by God who "dealt with him as a teacher instructing a pupil."[7] Ignatius describes five visions he experienced as part of his "training" that gave him a deeper understanding of the Trinity, creation, the Eucharist, and Our Lady.

There follows the narration of the most important spiritual experience of the whole of Ignatius's life: the climax of his growth in the things of God. Sitting by the Cardoner River, he tells us that he received an illumination that allowed him to see the world with new eyes and to find God in all things:

Ignatius's Roots; Ignatius's God

One day he went to the Church of St. Paul, situated about a mile from Manresa. Near the road is a stream, on the bank of which he sat, and gazed at the deep waters flowing by. While seated there, the eyes of his soul were opened. He did not have any special vision, but his mind was enlightened on many subjects, spiritual and intellectual.[8]

Commentators on the Ignatian text, in particular, Brian O'Leary, SJ, conclude that Ignatius "was seeing familiar realities in a new light and with a greater profundity"[9] so much so that he grasped what we call today the interconnectedness of all things. And that "their guiding principles and causes," were to be found in God, the Trinity. There was no longer any separation between the sacred and the secular.

BASQUE IDENTITY

It is possible that this spiritual experience had its cultural roots in the Basque identity of Ignatius:

> First impressions of the Basques suggest that they are tough, but then you discover their gentleness. They're a bit like rustic bread, which has a hard crust but is very sweet inside and seasoned with great feeling. Ignatius was certainly influenced by his background, for example, in his writing which can come across as very concise and dry but conceals a beautiful sensitivity that can help the reader develop an inner tenderness.

IGNATIUS WAS GREEN

Without doubt Ignatius was the product of his time, his family and his cultural entourage.[10]

The environment of the Basque region known as Gipuzkoa, the birthplace of St. Ignatius, is geographically a pocket of mountain and coast, boasting a rocky coastline, forests, and the granite crests of the Pyrenees mountains. Tomás Eceizabarrena, SJ, a Basque Jesuit friend, once told me that he believes that these mountains influenced the Basque character, endowing it with its strong, silent identity. In fact, on my visits to Loyola, I have always been struck by the very many trees and the various shades of green that surround it.

Ignatius grew up in a typical Basque agricultural society, nurtured and raised in the lap of nature by his wet-nurse, Maria Garín, and her family who lived in the tiny village of Eguibar, nestled in the valley not far from the castle. There, surrounded by abundant greenery, close to the meadows and mountains, the woods and the streams, Ignatius would have been acquainted with the flora and fauna of village life. There, as a true Basque, Ignatius cultivated a great fondness for the beauties and marvels of God's creation. That fondness stayed with him all his life. At Loyola during his convalescence, Iñigo would sit by the window at night and watch the stars. As he himself recalls: "It was my greatest consolation to gaze upon the heavens and the stars, which I often did, and for long stretches at a time, because when doing so I felt within myself a powerful urge to be serving our Lord."[11]

Ignatius never lost his Basque identity and all through his life he appreciated the countryside and nature that he found spiritually refreshing. We are told that

Ignatius's Roots; Ignatius's God

he began to seek God according to his ability and will but also with his heart. He would remain late beneath the stars, letting his eyes range over their shining forms, the work of God....His glance would stray from star to star, from one bright constellation to another even brighter, even more plunged into the heights of the cosmos and he was moved by the contemplation of the lines which one day the hand of God had traced in space. For the first time the firmament appeared to him as an immense act of love, and he thought of the divine sower who had scattered those mysterious points of light as the hand of man scatters the seeds of grain. The thought of God the Creator and Comforter must have been of enormous consolation to him, engaged as he was in a most difficult and painful uprooting of himself.[12]

Regarding his love of nature, we are also told that,

later in Rome, Ignatius would take visitors into the small garden, or orchard belonging to the house, to talk. It is said that he would often stop to look meditatively at the blue sky. Nadal says that Ignatius was able to see the Trinity in the leaf of an orange tree. Ribadeneira reports of the early companions' observations of Ignatius: We often saw how little things became an occasion for him to lift his spirit to God, and this—even the littlest things....The sight of a plant, flower, leaf, shrub or fruit, even a small insect, would set him off in contemplation.[13]

IGNATIUS WAS GREEN

Toward the end of his life, Ignatius devoted himself to writing the Constitutions of the Society of Jesus. The office where he wrote opened onto a balcony, from where he would gaze at the star-studded sky. Father Annibal Codretti observed: "The whole time that the Venerable Father Ignatius was composing he Constitutions during the seven months that I waited on him…when the weather was fine, in order to be less disturbed, he went into the garden which a Roman gentleman had lent to him for his use. A table was set there, on which were placed ink and paper, and so he wrote what came to his mind."[14]

In this context, Ignatius's life and spirituality took on an amazing simplicity: God becomes one, unrivaled, like the Basque mountain peaks and plains, stretching on and on, without break or change. God, Our Creator and Lord, is the God of the *Spiritual Exercises*.

3

GROWING THE TEXT OF THE *SPIRITUAL EXERCISES*

From the Seeds of His Journey

In Manresa he decided to write some notes in his little book.

—Ignatius of Loyola

The *Spiritual Exercises of St. Ignatius* were a lived experience before they were written notes, a text, or a published work. Ignatius "made" his *Spiritual Exercises* in Loyola and Manresa over a relatively short period of time, between 1521 and 1523. But the composition of the manuscript entitled the *Spiritual Exercises* was, in fact, the fruit of twenty-five years of Ignatius's personal experience combined with a similar period spent helping others. During that time, Ignatius crafted the text gradually, expanding, correcting, and polishing it. It was a process that included stops and starts, abandoned notes, interruptions, and unfinished sentences, involving not just one text but several, in both Spanish and Latin.[1] It was a writing process that spanned three different moments in his life, and happened in three different places: Manresa, Paris, and Rome.

THE SOURCES

The sources for the text of the *Spiritual Exercises* were twofold: first, Ignatius's own lived experience and the experience of others to whom he gave the *Exercises*; and second, the works of certain spiritual writers that Ignatius read avidly. As we noted in the previous chapter, Ignatius's spiritual experience and conversion began in May 1521, in the family castle in his native Azpeitia, where he was recuperating from the famous cannonball injury that he had sustained while fighting in the battle in Pamplona. His convalesce dragged on due to the painful "cosmetic surgery" demanded by Ignatius's vanity, yet relieved only by reading.[2]

The Life of Christ, one of the books he was given, was not just a biography of Jesus Christ but also a history and commentary borrowed from the Church fathers, together with a series of dogmatic and moral dissertations, spiritual instructions, meditations, and prayers. It had a significant influence on the development of Christian meditation—namely, stepping into and immersing oneself in a Gospel scene. Ludolph proposed a method of prayer that asks the reader to visualize events in Christ's life. He also had insights into the humanity of Jesus. Captivated by the attractive person of Jesus, Ignatius incorporated this method of praying using the Gospel scenes into the text of the *Spiritual Exercises*. In the second and third weeks of the *Exercises*, Ignatius suggests accompanying Jesus through his life, passion, and death by using our physical senses—sight, sound, taste, smell, and touch—to enter the events of Jesus's life and become part of them by placing oneself

Growing the Text of the *Spiritual Exercises*

in the scene and paying attention to the details, such as enjoying the Galilean countryside: "See the people...listen to what they are saying...watch what they are doing."[3] It is by being exposed to and losing oneself in the story, and listening to Jesus with our hearts and minds that we may get to know him better, love him more dearly, and follow him more nearly. The idea is simply to watch what Jesus does: to listen to how he speaks; note how people react to him; ponder his words; talk to him; and become part of his life. Indeed, the events in the life of Jesus form the backbone of the *Spiritual Exercises;* they contain more than forty exercises in which Ignatius offers imaginative ways of encountering the person of Jesus Christ.

At the same time, each chapter in the *Golden Legend* was about a different saint and was considered the closest thing to an encyclopedia of medieval saint lore. The author's purpose was to satisfy a public eager for a book which dealt, in an attractive style, with the saints of all times and places—their stories and their deeds, sufferings, and miracles. He sought to captivate, encourage, and edify the faithful by depicting the saints as knights of God dedicated to their Eternal Lord. Ignatius was certainly captivated by the stories, but above all, by those of Sts. Francis, Dominic, and Benedict. He was determined to emulate, even to "out-saint" the saints, doing what those heroic followers of Christ had done, and more.

Ignatius relates that "he greatly enjoyed his books, and the idea struck him to copy down, in abridged form, the more important items in the life of Christ and of the saints....The result of all this was that he felt within himself a strong impulse to serve our Lord."[4] That strong impulse and determination to do "more" was translated in the *Spiritual Exercises* into The Call of the Eternal King

IGNATIUS WAS GREEN

and the Meditation on Two Standards. Ignatius, who had defended Pamplona against the French, going far beyond the call of duty, now wanted to transfer his allegiance from his earthly king and to enlist in the ranks of the army of Christ the King, to labor with him in his mission "to conquer the whole world and all enemies,"[5] and to be counted among those who feel "greater desires to distinguish himself themselves by serving Him completely"[6]; asking to be placed under the standard of Jesus.[7]

Moreover, as he read and reflected on these books, Ignatius noticed a change taking place within him and he began to take notes of those interior movements he was experiencing:

> When he thought of worldly things it gave him great pleasure, but afterward he found himself dry and sad. But when he thought of journeying to Jerusalem, and of living only on herbs, and practicing austerities, he found pleasure not only while thinking of them, but also when he had ceased.[8]

So it was that, in his bedroom in Loyola, now called the Chapel of the Conversion, the sacred space where Ignatius recovered, raged, reconciled, and converted, Ignatius gave himself to God.[9]

MANRESA

With his convalescence and reading completed, and fresh from his life-changing encounter with Jesus Christ, the Eternal King, together with his commitment now to serve him, Ignatius set out to begin his new life in Manresa,

Growing the Text of the *Spiritual Exercises*

which became the context of both his spiritual apprenticeship and the crafting of the text of the *Exercises*.

Pope Francis reminds us that "the history of our friendship with God is always linked to particular places which take on an intensely personal meaning."[10] For Ignatius, that place was Manresa. He spent almost a year there in a cave, formed of naked rock, hollowed by the force of the wind and rain, and set in the characteristic Basque landscape of the area, looking out on the Cardoner River, and commanding a panoramic view of the rugged mountain range of Monserrat in the distance. It must have provided an ideal sanctuary where the nature-loving Basque aristocrat, who was falling in love with God, could receive his spiritual formation and the mystical experiences that would be essential for the *Spiritual Exercises*. St. Ignatius's cave in Manresa, (La Coveta), has now been transformed into a chapel. The painting on the door of the tabernacle depicts St. Ignatius present in a scene of the nativity. Ignatius, wrapped in contemplation, is keeling in front of the Virgin Mary, who is holding the Christ Child, while St. Joseph points to the infant Jesus. A discrete servant girl stands in the background also contemplating the Holy Family. Alongside Ignatius, on the floor, lays an open book—the text of the *Spiritual Exercises*. This picture symbolically illustrates how the cave at Manresa became identified as "the cradle" of Ignatius's Christ-centered *Spiritual Exercises*, in which the imaginative contemplation of biblical scenes is very important.

It was in Manresa that Ignatius decided to "write out some notes in his little book, which for his own consolation he carefully carried about with him."[11] We do not know the content of those notes, but we do know that out of this experience there would eventually come the text that

IGNATIUS WAS GREEN

we know as the *Spiritual Exercises*.[12] Ignatius insisted that it was in Manresa that the Lord took him by the hand and taught him as a teacher teaches a child; a learning process made up of many graces as well as spiritual trials.

The most famous and life-changing of those graces was a spiritual experience that took place toward the end of his stay in Manresa. In his *Autobiography*, he describes that extraordinary experience that took place about a mile from Manresa on the bank of a stream that we now know was the Cardoner River:

> While seated there, the eyes of his soul were opened. He did not have any special vision, but his mind was enlightened on many subjects, spiritual and intellectual. So clear was this knowledge that from that day everything appeared to him in a new light.[13]

Nothing would ever be the same again for Ignatius. He had a new mind and a new heart. Juan Polanco, his secretary, opined that what he saw in this experience by the river led directly to Ignatius's decision to write the *Spiritual Exercises*. Many Ignatian scholars think that the experience was the basis for the Contemplation to Gain Love at the end of the *Spiritual Exercises*. This meditation certainly has mystical overtones; it presents God, who is present in all things, who labors to transform creation, and who bathes all of creation in a ceaseless cascade of blessings and gifts, like the light radiating from the sun, bathing us in warmth, or the waters of God's tender generosity washing over us and soaking into our whole being, transforming our lives.

This experience beside the Cardoner was the climax of all the mystical graces that Ignatius received at Manresa.

Growing the Text of the *Spiritual Exercises*

Everything else paled in comparison. Nothing else would ever come even close. Ignatius writes: "So clear was this knowledge that from that day everything appeared to him in a new light. Such was the abundance of this light in his mind that all the divine helps received, and all the knowledge acquired up to his sixty-second year, were not equal to it."[14] The Cardoner experience formed a touchstone for his whole life and for the *Spiritual Exercises*.

Other Sources

In Manresa, Ignatius found two more books which influenced both his own spiritual experience and his writing of the *Spiritual Exercises*. The first was the *Compedio Breve del Ejercitatorio de la via espiritual* (Brief Compendium of the Book of Exercises for the Spiritual Life) by the Benedictine Abbott of the Abbey of Monserrat from which Ignatius learned the importance of a method of procedure that would later structure the *Spiritual Exercises*.[15] The second was *The Imitation of Christ* by Thomas à Kempis. Reading the *Imitation* had a profound effect on Ignatius, so much so that he later commented that "he never wished to read any other devotional books."[16] Moreover, he recommended the *Imitation* as spiritual reading appropriate to the second week of the *Exercises*: "It is profitable to spend occasional periods in reading from *The Imitation of Christ*, the Gospels or lives of the saints."[17]

THE PROCESS OF DEVELOPMENT

Ignatius never intended his *Spiritual Exercises* as a book to be read but rather as a collection of notes, a manual of norms not for the person making the retreat, but for

IGNATIUS WAS GREEN

the director who is to provide a "method and procedure" for the person making the *Exercises*. From the moment he left his home in Loyola, Ignatius began to converse with people on spiritual topics, proposing methods of prayer that he himself had already experienced, and continued to give various spiritual exercises during his travels from then on. The collected experience of all those people also enabled Ignatius to continuing honing the text of the *Exercises*. Already in Manresa, and later in Paris, Barcelona, Alcalá, and Salamanca, he encouraged people he met to practice his *Exercises*. Then, while in Rome, Ignatius continued to give the *Exercises* to people from all walks of life. which enabled him to continue to fine-tune them.

In Alcalá, Ignatius was questioned by the Inquisition about his "spiritual conversations" and the "exercises" he was giving. That encounter impressed on him the need for more theological formation to help souls more profoundly. So, in 1528, he arrived in Paris where six years of reading, study, classes, and exams awaited him. There he gained a theological framework to undergird the spiritual exercises that he had been giving for years. He also read the works of the spiritual masters in the patristic tradition: St. Augustine, St. Gregory, St. Bernard, St. Thomas Aquinas, and the twelfth-century theologian, Peter Lombard.

After completing his studies in Paris, Ignatius once again took up his incomplete notes, the embryo of his future *Exercises*, to make further additions and corrections, in the light of his growing spiritual experience.

But it was Rome, a city built on the river Tiber and surrounded by seven hills, that was to be the final stop in Ignatius's earthly pilgrim's journey. There, toward the end of his life, he made his final additions and completed the definitive text of the *Spiritual Exercises*, in the light of his growing spiritual experience. Ignatius fine-tuned them to stretch the mind, the heart, and the soul for the greater glory of God and the loving service of others to make, what we would call today, a positive difference in our world.

So it was that the creation-loving Basque, embraced by nature, put the final touches on the *Exercises*, which were finally approved by Pope Paul III for publication in 1548.

AN AFFECTIVE SPIRITUALITY

At the same time, Ignatius wrote and gave the *Exercises* in the rich social, cultural, and religious context of late medieval Spanish spirituality, which undoubtedly influenced him and can be detected in various moments in the text. It was a spirituality inspired by the spirit of the "reconquest," an urgency to reach out toward and embrace the "infinite" together with a militaristic spirit of adventure and action, that accompanied knights on the battlefield—or Ignatius, as he led the resistance of the besieged city of Pamplona—and added a lively passion to popular devotion. It was an affective spirituality centered on the humanity of the crucified Christ, hanging on the cross, and on identification with Christ's suffering.

In one sense, there is nothing "new" in the *Exercises*. Ignatius relied on prayer forms and spiritual traditions deeply rooted in Christianity. What is original, however, is the way in which Ignatius skillfully weaves them together. The *Spiritual Exercises* were never meant to be read as, for example, were the works of Bonaventure. They are, rather, an essentially experiential and practical "how to" manual or guide. They were meant to be "given" and "received" or lived by the director and the retreatant. According to Louis

IGNATIUS WAS GREEN

M. Savary,[18] *The Spiritual Exercises of St. Ignatius of Loyola* were an revolutionary document for their time. In the text, St. Ignatius introduced new structured methods of prayer, well-ordered steps for meditation, guidelines for contemplation, a systemized set of rules for spiritual directors and retreatants, methods of discernment, and an approach to the daily examination of conscience.

But the dimension that Ignatius did bring to the *Exercises* was his understanding of creation—his relationship with God, Our Creator and Lord, and all created things. Ignatius recognized how profoundly loved we are by God through God's creation, that both teaches and sustains us; an awareness that permeated the whole text; an insight that he offered to the Church of his time, a Church badly in need of conversion. With the *Spiritual Exercises*, Ignatius gave the Church both a means of renewal and a spiritual adventure. They did not offer a theory or speculative theological treatise, but rather an individual journey, based on his own pilgrim experience. For Ignatius, the *Exercises* were a testament of God's gentle and persistent "laboring"[19] in his life. He was convinced that they could help other people draw closer to God and discern God's call in their lives, as they had in his. But the *Exercises* were never meant for the Jesuits alone. St. Ignatius crafted them as a layman and intended them to benefit the whole Church. What Martin Luther tried to do from outside, Ignatius sought to accomplish from within the Catholic Church.

THE FINAL TEXT

Each section of the final text of the *Exercises*—from the Principle and Foundation at the start to the Contemplation to Gain Love, the two bookends of the *Exercises*—

Growing the Text of the *Spiritual Exercises*

whether penned in Manresa, Paris, or Rome was the result of Ignatius's own experience of the threefold relationship among God, human beings, and the rest of creation. Fr. Peter-Hans Kolvenbach, the former General of the Society of Jesus, points out that "these three relationships are, for Ignatius, so closely united that a person cannot find God unless he finds him through the environment, and conversely, that his relationship to the environment will be out of balance unless he also relates to God."[20]

The *Exercises* begin with an "Annotation," recommending both the retreatant and director "to allow the Creator to deal immediately with the creature and the creature with its Creator and Lord."[21] The *Exercises* then move into a natural rhythm and are divided into four weeks. These are not calendar weeks, but rather interconnected movements experienced by the retreatant. First is a time of preparation, the Principle and Foundation, during which the retreatant is invited to consider who we are and the gift of God's ongoing creation in the world and in us. The idea of radical spiritual freedom is also introduced. Having experienced God's boundless generosity, we also experience our own limited response; the retreatant moves into the First Week, and the experience of being loved and embraced as a sinner. The Second Week concentrates on the person of Christ in the Gospel—who for Ignatius is also the cosmic Christ—who calls us to discipleship by seeking to know Christ more intimately, to love him more passionately, and to follow him more closely. The Third Week is about a deepening personal identification with the suffering Christ, and a sharing in his passion together with that of humanity and the earth. In the Fourth Week, we walk with the risen Lord, "finding God in all things,"[22] and committing ourselves to serving God and others. The culmination of this week and indeed of the entire process of the *Exercises* is found in the final meditation, the Contemplation to Gain Love that offers a tender way to be loved and to love, bathed in God's radiant light.

Finally, the discernment of spirits, which forms part of the appendix, underpins the whole expanse of the *Exercises*. Here, Ignatius affirms again that we cannot have knowledge of God apart from the created world. He says that consolation is "an interior movement…aroused in the soul, by which it is inflamed with love of its Creator and Lord, and as a consequence, can love no created thing on the face of the earth for its own sake, but only in the Creator of them all."[23]

4

GOD'S DREAM FOR US

The Principle and Foundation

The world is charged with the grandeur of God.

—Gerard Manley Hopkins

Ignatius knew from his experience of guiding others through the *Exercises* that the spiritual adventure he offered "to overcome oneself and to order one's life"[1] needed adequate preparation. He composed a list of everything that both those giving and those receiving the *Exercises* needed to pack before setting out on this journey—all the appropriate dispositions needed for the long journey ahead—for the fourfold conversation that would follow among the director, the retreatant, God, and all creation. These dispositions included generosity, objectivity, awe, and trust, as we are held tenderly in the embrace of God, the creator of surprises. He called this list the Annotations.

Ignatius also knew that a journey needs a starting point and a roadmap to guide us to our destination—the end of the journey—to where we want to go and who we want to be. That is what crafts our personal, unrepeatable, surprising narrative. God's dream for us: our vocation,

IGNATIUS WAS GREEN

identity, and mission. What Ignatius called the Principle and Foundation provides the basis for all that happens in the *Exercises*, and acts as a refrain that is repeated throughout every stage in the Ignatian process.

We do not know when the Principle and Foundation or the Annotations of the *Spiritual Exercises* were written. It may have been when Ignatius was studying in Paris. In 1535, Fr. John Heylar, an Englishman and secretary to Cardinal Pole, spent some time in Paris, where he made the *Exercises* with either Ignatius himself or Peter Favre, as his director. Those *Exercises* contain both the Principle and Foundation and several Annotations, describing the dispositions necessary to receive the *Exercises*—the very same dispositions which enabled St. Ignatius to live his spiritual experiences in Manresa and which filled his mind and heart as he sat on the banks of the Cardoner River. "It is very helpful to him who is receiving the Exercises to enter into them with great courage and generosity towards his Creator and Lord, offering Him all his will and liberty, that His Divine Majesty may make use of his person and of all he has according to His most Holy Will."[2]

The final twenty Annotations were probably added to the text of the *Exercises* later, when St. Ignatius, then in Rome, began to entrust the giving of the *Exercises* to others, who would need to be trained in the art of offering this Ignatian spiritual experience. The function of the Annotations was, and is, to equip the director to present the *Exercises*. The opening words of the Annotations indicate the importance Ignatius gave to them as affording an overall understanding of the *Exercises*: "Annotations to give some understanding of the spiritual exercises which follow, and to enable him who is to give and him who is to receive them to help themselves."[3]

God's Dream for Us

THE ANNOTATIONS

The importance of the Annotations is embedded in their theological foundation, which is none other than the indispensable relationship between our freedom and God's grace. According to the text of St. Ignatius, the *Exercises* are both "given" and "received." They are "given," but delicately, as if they were "kisses blown" by God, Our Creator and Lord. The same God who lovingly imagined us into existence and gave us the earth as our home, and all other creatures as our family, is a God who seduces and "embraces us" in the *Exercises*.[4] It is this same God who pampers us, caressing us in and through the whole of creation, and caresses and enfolds the retreatants in the arms of his creative and redemptive love. All the retreatants have to do is to "receive," to allow themselves to be embraced and drawn into a relationship with God and all created things. This ecological insight, subtly hinted at in the Annotations is unpacked fully in the Principle and Foundation of the first week.

Based on his illumination at the Cardoner River that all creatures come from God and return to God, and inspired by the first chapters of Genesis, Ignatius wants to make it abundantly clear at the outset of the *Exercises* that the focus is on God not on us—God the Creator—the God who wanted someone and something else to love, someone and something else to gift into existence and to relate to, and someone and something that would reflect his glory—the God who created everyone and everything. Then, and only then, Ignatius turns his attention to the retreatant—to us. Who we are? Why we are here? What is the purpose for which we were created, the project that God dreams for us? We human beings, he says, are created. We are part of the whole of creation. We are from God and for God, dependent on God, called to be co-creators with God, and partners in God's cosmic plan.

In the biblical creation narrative, there are three closely related protagonists: God, humanity, and the earth, from which humanity is fashioned. We find the same relationship at the very beginning of the *Spiritual Exercises*: God, Our Creator and Lord, humanity, and all the other things on the face of the earth. God's work of creation reveals an innate and intimate inter-relationship that existed between them from the very beginning when God, Our Creator and Lord, created everything—a *divine milieu* in which everything that exists, "lives and moves and has its being" (cf. Acts 17:28). An awesome sacramentality, exquisitely captured in the words of Teilhard de Chardin:

> Glorious Lord Christ: the divine influence secretly diffused and active in the depths of matter, and the dazzling centre where all the innumerable fibres of the multiple meet; power as implacable as the world and as warm as life; you whose forehead is of the whiteness of snow, whose eyes are of fire, and whose feet are brighter than molten gold; you whose hands imprison the stars; you who are the first and the last, the living and the dead and the risen again; you who gather into your exuberant unity every beauty, every affinity, every energy, every mode of existence; it is you to whom my being cried out with a desire as vast as the universe.[5]

THE PRINCIPLE AND FOUNDATION

In the Principle and Foundation, Ignatius clearly states that God has a comprehensive plan for all creation: "[The

God's Dream for Us

human person] is created to praise, reverence, and serve God Our Lord….And the other things on the face of the earth are created for [human beings] and that they may help [them] in prosecuting the end for which [they are] created."[6] The purpose of our lives is to be "wow people," who live in love with God and others, both here now on earth and in heaven forever. God made everything else to move us closer toward his love, recognizing that everything is God's gift to us, delighting in everything for that very reason, praising God, and longing to serve God in and through all other things.

Ignatius goes on to imply that we are invited to be involved in and cooperate with the adventure of what God is doing in the world. We are challenged to participate in the divine vision: namely, a world where human beings live in friendship and harmony with God, with other human beings, and with the whole of creation:

> From this it follows that man is to use them as much as they help him on to his end, and ought to rid himself of them so far as they hinder him as to it.
>
> For this it is necessary to make ourselves indifferent to all created things in all that is allowed to the choice of our free will and is not prohibited to it; so that, on our part, we want not health rather than sickness, riches rather than poverty, honor rather than dishonor, long rather than short life, and so in all the rest; desiring and choosing only what is most conducive for us to the end for which we are created.[7]

This implies letting God love us just as we are, and so making the statement that God is the only Absolute,

IGNATIUS WAS GREEN

and that everything else is secondary. The realization that everything that happens to us—health or sickness, wealth or poverty, honor or dishonor, and long or short life— is all part of God's plan and finds its meaning only in that context. It is living more fully what God made us to be—family, sons, and daughters—who adore the Father, celebrating our relationship with God in and through our relationship with all created things, and wanting only to do God's will.

Hence, from the very beginning of the *Exercises*, the retreatant is plunged into a context "charged," as Gerard Manley Hopkins would say, "with the grandeur of God,"[8] and thrust into the presence of a loving Creator-God who, long before we came into existence, gifted each one of us with creation to be our home, in which everything, according to St. Ignatius, is created so that we might come to know and serve God more deeply and creatively. Gerald M. Fagin holds that:

> Ignatius believed that anyone who prayerfully considers the basic truth that we are created out of love by a transcendent God of holiness will grow in a sense of reverence. We will have a deepened sense of the sacredness of all things if we think of everything as continually being called and sustained in being by God. We will stand in awe not just before sunsets and mountains, flowers and trees, but also, and especially, before every person we meet. Reverence is a disposition of a heart that allows us to live before the beauty and goodness of every creature and the God who made them. In Ignatian terminology, reverence will enable us to find God in all things.[9]

God's Dream for Us

On the contrary, the rupture of this relationship or the failure to recognize the material world as God's dwelling place not only prevents us from discovering God but results in a dysfunctional relationship with both God and the rest of creation that, in turn, leads to the manipulative exploitation of creation that lies at the root of the present-day ecological crisis.

It is interesting and attests to the contemporary relevance of the Principle and Foundation that there are so many *contemporary* readings of the Ignatian text. David Fleming's reading of the Principle and Foundation is possibly the most well-known and the one used by many spiritual directors.

In 2011, however, the Australian Jesuit, John Reilly, SJ, offered the following version:

> As Christians we believe we come from a loving God who freely creates us to discover the mystery of God's love in our lives.
>
> We believe God creates all things that we may find in them God's presence and energy by learning to share our lives with other people and care for our kinship with all that wonderfully shares and supports our lives.
>
> We find the beauty and mystery of our human lives, therefore, only by choosing, insofar as it is left to our free choice, what helps to share our lives in love, not what hinders this.
>
> For the freedom to love we need to hold ourselves open to all things—wealth or poverty, fame or disgrace, health or sickness, a long life or a short one, and to all else.

IGNATIUS WAS GREEN

> We need to let God grace us into a spiritual freedom, gratefully responsive to God's prior love in our lives, to desire and choose what better helps us live the love for which God made us.[10]

Complementing this approach, Louis Savary presents the Principle and Foundation as God's invitation to all humanity to be active cocreators in God's evolutionary project:

> You were created to make a unique contribution to the great evolutionary project initiated and continually supported by God, namely bringing all creation together into one magnificent conscious loving union.
>
> Since all other created things in the universe share with you this common eternal destiny, they are essential to and inseparable from you as you participate in the pursuit of that on-going evolutionary process.
>
> Individually and with others, you are to use all means available to promote and carry out this shared purpose with all your personal creativity, compassion and energy, always seeking and choosing what is more conducive to that purpose.
>
> For this, God empowers you to grow in passionate love and care for all elements of the cosmos, since they, as you, all live and move and have their being in God's love.[11]

Savary's translation evokes Caitlin Matthews's reinterpretation of the biblical creation narrative written in terms of ecospirituality:

God's Dream for Us

In the beginning, God sang everything alive. God sang the sky, the land and the seas. God sang the plants and trees. God sang the moon, the sun and the stars. God sang the animals to live in the sea, in the sky and on the Earth.... Then God, Mother and Father of All, sang of Man and Woman. God said to them, "This Earth is your garden. The rocks, the plants, trees and animals are your family. Go and explore your home." The Man and the Woman thanked God. They greeted every stone, plant, tree and animal. They learned what each living thing could do.... The Man and the Woman sat together and watched the stars grow bright in the sky. Then the Woman said to God, "Everything in the garden has their special gift. The squirrel can jump, the snake can crawl, the bird can fly. What is our special gift?" And God answered, "In all the world, you and the Man are most like me. You have a special duty. You will care for everything on Earth. Your special gift is to learn and to care."[12]

The Principle and Foundation initiates the pulse of this collaborative rhythm. It is the introduction to the four-week dynamic of the *Exercises* that follows—the refrain running through each of the weeks that nurtures an ever-deepening experience of the caring presence of God, Our Creator and Lord.

5

CREATION HOLDS ITS BREATH

The First Week

> *An exclamation of wonder with deep feeling, going through all creatures.*
>
> —*Spiritual Exercises* (60)

Having gazed with awe at God's dream for humanity—God's grace and surprising promise for each of us as expressed in the Principle and Foundation—Ignatius now leads us into a contemplation of the interruption of that narrative by sin. Sin can only be understood in the light of grace, of what was meant to be, and only God can allow us to comprehend the reality of sin.

At first sight, the five exercises that make up the First Week of the *Exercises* are a little disconcerting. It seems that they present a series of very dry and abstract reflections in a language that today presents difficulties in the light of recent exegesis and current theology. Or, that they present, at least, a veritable obstacle course that, once mastered, allows the retreatant—with a sigh of relief—to enter, finally, into the remainder of the *Spiritual Exercises*. The spiritual intuition of St. Ignatius that underpins these *Exercises* is very different. In fact, embedded in the text of this First Week is an amazingly intense and very real affective experience that balances shame and consolation. It is an experience that happens in the heart rather than the mind, a heart that beats to the rhythm of the earth.

Just like the Principle and Foundation, the First Week mirrors the biblical vision that creation is good and human beings are gardeners, divinely commissioned to cultivate and care for the earth. But then, human beings wanted to be gods, not just gardeners, and sin entered the world—collective sin, as a condition rather than a series of wrongdoings; what Martin Luther King Jr., called "the gone-wrongness of human nature."[1]

The First Week focuses on the experience of sin, but it is also about so much more, for sin is not the end of the story. The First Week is about sin in the context of God's love. The end of the story is about what happens when sin and love meet. The sin of the creature is interrupted by the love of God, the Creator; the creature who has sinned is held constantly in being and rocked tenderly in the arms of God's creative love. This experience draws the retreatant into the dynamic of knowing oneself as a sinner, but a sinner that is passionately loved by God—a sinful creature, loved by our Creator and Lord, and loved specifically through God's creation. Above all, it centers on the utterly moving tenderness and compassion of Christ, our Redeemer, whose embrace is forgiveness. In this way, Ignatius encourages the retreatant to move from an awareness of sin and our complicity in sin to conversion and transformation that overflows with a heartfelt gratitude for being loved by God.

IGNATIUS WAS GREEN

The challenge of the First Week is to come to an understanding and acceptance of the reality of sin and its impact. The meditations and contemplations that make up this First Week are experienced alongside a growing consciousness of the oneness of the human race and with the whole of creation enable the retreatant to grapple with the mystery of evil and grasp the "disorder" in humanity and in our world caused by the sins of humanity. "Disorder" is the term that Ignatius used for what modern Ignatian scholars refer to as the "dysfunctional relationship between us and God and the rest of Creation."[2] Pope Francis described that relationship vividly in 2016, in a document coinciding the World Day of Prayer for Creation, where, in speaking about the devastation of the environment, he says that "God gave us a bountiful garden, but we have turned it into a polluted wasteland of 'debris, desolation and filth.'"[3]

To a twenty-first–century reader, the breakdown of the First Week of the *Exercises* might seem quaint and vaguely reminiscent of a novel by Dan Brown, packed with apocalyptic imagery such as angels, Adam and Eve, demons and hellfire, but a Jesuit reflection on ecology and Ignatian spirituality brings this First Week firmly into the present:

> The rebellion of Adam and Eve explains the contemporary disrespect for the Creator, which spills over into mistreatment of fellow human beings and recklessness with the rest of creation.... The gravity of sin consists precisely in its undermining and destroying the foundational relationship of God, man and created things. Ignatius would have each one of us sense, taste and feel sin in its horror and destructiveness, and as each one

Creation Holds Its Breath

of us is involved, we meditate in the first person. For with my sin I partake of, become one with, a history of de-creation, a story of death and hell.[4]

In the first exercise of the First Week, Ignatius begins the narrative of how sin and evil irrupted into history by directing our gaze toward a cosmic horizon—to the sin "out there"—the evil that permeates our world and its political, economic, social, and cultural structures. A careful reading of the apparently simplistic, biblically inspired, Ignatian text recalls the revealed history of sin as recounted in the last and first books of God's Word—the sin of the angels in the Book of Revelation, and that of Adam and Eve in the Book of Genesis. The affective responses provoked by this narrative move from a growing, intense shame, to dismay and utter horror in the face of evil; a zero tolerance of all its forms. Ignatius clarifies that sin is always "against one's Creator and Lord." The angels had "forgotten" that they were created beings—creatures: "I say to bring to memory the sin of the Angels, how they, being created in grace, not wanting to help themselves with their liberty to reverence and obey their Creator and Lord."[5] Sin is, therefore, a rupture of the relationship between Creator and creature both in heaven and on earth.

That second rupture takes place in a garden, a paradise on earth, where Adam was placed after he was created, formed from the dust of the earth. The divine Gardener relationally and lovingly breathed his own life into Adam's lungs. Then the Gardener planted his garden and gave it to Adam, to humanity, to care for both plants and animals, while remaining intimately involved with the garden and its inhabitants, walking through it, and conversing with them. Adam, along with and Eve, who is created when no

IGNATIUS WAS GREEN

other creature is a suitable helper for Adam, are destined to share God's task of caring for the garden, based on trust and the mutual relationship of Creator and creature that God has initiated with them. But they reject the terms that God has placed on that relationship.

In the third exercise, Ignatius invites us to consider our personal sin in the wider context of the actions of the whole of humanity. He redirects our gaze from the contemplation of "sin out there" to taking a hard look at our own personal sin in all its aspects—word, deed, and omission—the gap between God's dream for us and our reality; who and what we might have been and who we are now; the lost opportunities to encounter and bond with God, others, and the rest of creation. But then, this exercise suddenly tumbles into a modern understanding of the interconnectedness of all things. We are confronted by the conviction that creation is a living organism of interdependent systems and humanity's inseparable relationship with the earth and all the other beings that inhabit it—a continually evolving intertwined life force wrapped in the wonder of God.

The third exercise invites the retreatant to "look at who I am…in comparison to all men."[6] These "social forces" that engender injustice and exploitation are not vague, anonymous abstractions. Throughout the *Exercises*, we are reminded that they are human actions, their authors have names and faces. The retreatant is invited to discover his or her own face among the myriad faces that make up humanity, and set in the context of a particular time and space.

> To bring to memory all the sins of my life, looking from year to year, or from period to period. For this, three things are helpful: first, to look at the

place and the house where I have lived; second, the relations I have had with others; third, the occupations in which I have lived.[7]

Commenting on this text, Ricardo Antoncich, SJ, claims that the social dimension inherent in the First Week of the *Exercises* does not reflect an explicit intention by Ignatius to ascribe a social character to sin, but rather, is dictated by and consistent with his holistic anthropology. For Ignatius, the human person is both an integrated and universal whole, in whom the personal and the social are intrinsically united. For Ignatius, Antoncich argues, the singularity of the individual person is never enclosed in itself but is permanently open to the universality of all humanity.

He goes as far as to say that the *Exercises* remind us that even the most intimate and decisive moments of our personal lives happen in the context of the world around us, and that our own individual actions are also part of all human activity and therefore, always have a universal character. For Ignatius, it is not possible to feel responsible for the evil in our own lives without also accepting our coresponsibility for the evil in the world, including the present-day destruction of our planet. Social sin and personal sin are inextricably bound together. We are involved in social sin, whether we like it or not, and we contribute to its continued existence by our choices and our inactivity, notably today, by our failure to address the climate crisis.

The fifth point of the second exercise brings us to the edge of our seats, transfixed with awe and amazement:

> The fifth, a cry of wonder with deep feeling, going through all creatures, how they have left me in life and preserved me in it; the Angels,

IGNATIUS WAS GREEN

how, though they are the sword of the Divine Justice, they have endured me, and guarded me, and prayed for me; the Saints, how they have been engaged in interceding and praying for me; and the heavens, sun, moon, stars, and elements, fruits, birds, fishes and animals—and the earth, how it has not opened to swallow me up, creating new Hells for me to suffer in them forever![8]

This is a cry of wonder accompanied by a surge of emotion as the retreatant considers all creatures—in Franciscan terms, "brother sun and sister moon"—and the rest of the family who, despite our sinfulness, continues to nourish and protect us. Ignatius invites us to marvel as the earth—"our mother and our sister"[9]—sings her song of blessing and forgiveness; the song of the mercy of God, our Creator and Lord, bringing us to a "Colloquy of mercy."[10]

The Ignatian text finds an echo once again in the words of Caitlin Matthews: "On the path of wonder, you will again remember when you were sung from the earth. When you see the moon and the stars at night, or the sun sparkling in the water, when you hear the birds singing in the trees, when you hear the song of creation…You will remember that you are part of everything."[11]

The power of that memory brings us to our knees before Christ crucified in a colloquy that centers on God as the protagonist in our transformation, while our sin becomes an opportunity for discipleship rather than an obstacle. "Imagining Christ our Lord present and placed on the Cross, let me make a Colloquy, how from Creator He is come to making Himself man, and from life eternal is come to temporal death, and so to die for my sins."[12]

Finally, Ignatius suggests three questions as we kneel

there: "What have I done? What am I doing? and What will I do?" These questions encompass both the sin of the past and the good to be accomplished in the future—the longing to renew our following of Christ and develop our relationship with the rest of creation. Jesus on the cross bears the weight of evil—of both social and personal sin—but as Creator and Lord, he embraces the retreatant in the most intimate experience of being a sinner but a sinner who has been lovingly forgiven, one who can start again.

The First Week of the *Exercises*, then, focusses on sin, especially the systemic concept that we call "social sin": the all-pervasive, global nature of sin together with our complicity. The rupture of all relationships with God, with one another, and with creation. From the beginning of time sin, including our personal sin, has had a profoundly negative affect on the wounded earth and its broken people. This dual suffering is heard both in the cry of the poor and the groans of plundered nature. Ignatius tells us not to look away but to face the brokenness of our world. This, he says, is not God's dream, for God delights in the redemption and full flourishing of creation. In this context, the *Exercises* offer a path to "ecological conversion."[13]

6

THE CREATOR STEPS INTO CREATION

The Second Week

> *Hear what the Divine Persons are saying, that is: "Let Us work the redemption of the Human race."*
>
> —*Spiritual Exercises* (107)

After experiencing the depth of ecological sin, both systemic and personal, in the First Week of the *Exercises*, the Second Week invites the retreatant to enter into the mystery of the incarnation and to contemplate the earthly life of Jesus through praying the Gospel stories. The Ignatian dynamic focuses on the humanity of Christ and emphasizes that the created world is the place to experience God. Jesus Christ was born in a concrete time and place and, therefore, shares with us a deep relationship with life, nature, and the air that we breathe.

In the Gospel, we meet the God who became incarnate, who became a creature in the person of Jesus of Nazareth, and in whose life the natural world played an important role. He was born surrounded by animals and

The Creator Steps into Creation

grew up in a rural environment, intimately familiar with nature. Jesus talked about the Father as "Lord of heaven and earth" and likened the kingdom to the pageant of created things. Jesus told stories about weeds and wheat, the birds of the air, and the flowers of the fields; foxes and fish, trees and shrubs, lambs and wolves, sunrise, and the night sky. Jesus prayed in the hills and on mountaintops, in the desert and in the garden. Jesus walked alongside the bank of the river Jordan and on the shore of the Sea of Galilee.

The Second Week begins with a change of rhythm. We move from the Christ-centered colloquy that concludes the First Week to two introductory meditations that open the Christ-centered theme of the Second Week. These meditations open a door allowing the forgiven sinner to move from conversion to mission, from gratitude to hearing the call to collaborate with Christ, and to a new relationship with God and the world—both the human and the more-than-human-world. They are The Call of Christ the King, or The Kingdom,[1] and The Incarnation.

THE CALL OF CHRIST THE KING

The meditation on The Call of Christ the King is cosmic. The retreatant is invited to "to see Christ our Lord, King eternal, and before Him all the entire world" and to listen to his call:

> It is My will to conquer all the world and all enemies and so to enter into the glory of My Father; therefore, whoever would like to come with Me is to labor with Me, that following Me in the pain, he may also follow Me in the glory.[2]

IGNATIUS WAS GREEN

The "world," whose course is driven by God's dream is still unfinished, and Christ wants us human beings to be part of his plan—to join him in his project to renew the whole of creation. The call is to partnership with Christ— and a new relationship with him, is emphasized by the phrase "with me" which is repeated three times in the text. As noted earlier, the divine cosmic plan is expressed movingly in St. John's Gospel: "For God so loved the world that he gave his only Son, so that everyone who believes in him may not perish but may have eternal life. Indeed, God did not send the Son into the world to condemn the world, but in order that the world might be saved through him" (3:16–17).

Ignatius expects this meditation on the kingdom to evoke passionate commitment—a radical yes to be part of Christ's cosmic plan. In the Ignatian text, that yes is framed as a total self-giving, an oblation to the "King Eternal and universal Lord"[3] in the presence of the whole heavenly court:

> Eternal Lord of all things, I make my oblation with Thy favor and help, in presence of Thy infinite Goodness and in presence of Thy glorious Mother and of all the Saints of the heavenly Court; that I want and desire, and it is my deliberate determination, if only it be Thy greater service and praise, to imitate Thee in bearing all injuries and all abuse and all poverty of spirit, and actual poverty, too, if Thy most Holy Majesty wants to choose and receive me to such life and state.[4]

As in the First Week, Ignatius implies that such decisions, though personal, are not private matters, but have a universal dimension. First, they reflect our relationship with the community of saints, angels, and heavenly powers;

The Creator Steps into Creation

and second, they involve us in God's salvific work that embraces the whole of humanity—past, present, and future—together with the rest of creation.

Louis Savary makes the additional point that "Ignatius does not identify the Kingdom with the Roman Catholic Church, but sees Christ's reign as much more expansive, including all people and the entire world."[5] In the context of the seventeenth century, this universal vision is indeed noteworthy. Transferring Ignatius's meditation into our modern context, Savary suggests that Teilhard de Chardin, the French Jesuit paleontologist, might ask us to imagine "ten thousand" earthly leaders, rather than the "temporal king" of the Ignatian text:

> Men and women, spread all over the cities and villages of the Earth, people of all races and classes and religions and no religion, young and old, rich and poor, in store fronts and boardrooms, in homes and churches, in classrooms and picket lines, in jungles and around campfires, in laboratories and offices who represent ten thousand different caring groups, all rising above their daily difficulties. Finding ten thousand different ways to improve Earth and the beings on it.[6]

That universal mission is sketched out more fully in the following *Exercise*. The retreatant is invited to enter into God's viewpoint and contemplate the "whole expanse of the entire world and all the people in it"[7] with the loving gaze of our trinitarian God:

> Looking upon our world: men and women being born and being laid to rest, some getting married

IGNATIUS WAS GREEN

and others getting divorced, the old and the young, the rich and the poor, the happy and the sad, so many people aimless, despairing, hateful, and killing, so many undernourished, sick, and dying, so many struggling with life and blind to any meaning. With God, I can hear people laughing and crying, some shouting and screaming, some praying, others cursing.[8]

THE INCARNATION

Ignatius then invites the retreatant to listen to the Father, Son, and Spirit as they decide that God will interrupt the narrative of evil and open a new page in history, by becoming human and entering the world: "The leap of divine joy: God knows that the time has come when the mystery of salvation, hidden from the beginning of the world, will shine into human darkness and confusion. It is as if I can hear the Divine Persons saying, 'Let us work the redemption of the whole human race; let us respond to the groaning of all creation.'"[9] The Trinity's response is that God the Son will become a creature, will be born into the world, taking human flesh as Jesus of Nazareth, and becoming *Emmanuel*, "God-with-us." The Trinity's plan is the incarnation.

The mystery of the incarnation plunges us into the incredible depths of the love of a Creator God who becomes a creature; an eternal God confined in time and space; an almighty God wrapped in swaddling clothes, tiny and vulnerable; an unchanging God, who developed and grew "in wisdom and in years, and in divine and human favor" (Luke 2:52). God, the relational matrix that we know as Father, Son, and Spirit, and who sustains all of creation in a web of relationships becomes a human being, like us, interconnected with every other particle of creation: all of us made from stardust.

THE NATIVITY

Ignatius leads us to contemplate the Gospel account of the human conception and birth of God the Son, Jesus Christ, in the stable in Bethlehem. Ignatius proposes a series of Gospel contemplations, using our imagination and five senses to become present to the magic of each scene—watching and listening; touching and tasting—taking in the scene of the Holy Family, lulled by the rustle of the straw, the smell and the breath of the animals in the stable, and the crying of a newborn child, and seeing the stars bright in the night sky as the shepherds huddled, watching their sheep. We contemplate the ordinary framework and rhythm of the everyday life of Jesus's world in Nazareth that kneaded and shaped his maturing into adulthood.

THE PUBLIC LIFE OF JESUS

The *Exercises* move on to the contemplation of the public life of Jesus, mindful always "to ask for interior knowledge of the Lord, Who for me has become man, that I may more love and follow Him,"[10] who teaches and heals, and preaches the good news to the poor. In his teaching, Jesus uses many agricultural images and, in doing so, he teaches a new way of relating to nature. For the "ecological Jesus," the world was alive with God. All created things spoke to him of the Father; they mirrored God's creative love. The birds and the flowers sing the song of God's caring providence: "Look at the birds of the air: they neither sow

IGNATIUS WAS GREEN

nor reap nor gather into barns; and yet our heavenly Father feeds them....Consider the lilies of the field, how they grow; they neither toil nor spin, yet I tell you, that even Solomon in all his glory was not clothed like one of these" (Matt 6:26, 28–29). For Jesus, the sun and the rain that fall on all indiscriminately—on the just and the unjust—tell the story of a God who loves unconditionally. Jesus often described the kingdom or reign of God in terms of nature. He likened it to a mustard seed (Matt 13:31). Mark recounts the parable of the soil emphasizing the importance of the right type of soil for the growth of the sown seed and for a successful harvest (cf. Mark 4:1–9), while the parable of the growing seed stresses the natural process that finally culminates in the harvest (cf. Mark 4:26). The parables of Jesus and their various images not only speak of the essential role of nature in making the earth fertile, but also in revealing the presence of God in the natural world and Jesus's delight in the wonder of creation.

The Second Week of the *Exercises* invites us to know our eternal King and the mission to which he calls us by focusing on the person of Jesus Christ in the Gospel. Through the meditations, Ignatius helps us to simply be with Jesus, to accompany him, as the disciples did, to get to know him and his mission through his daily life. We watch and listen not only to what he says and does but to the tone of Jesus's voice—the nuances, attitude, and perspective—the gentleness of his touch, and the compassion in his eyes. The Second Week offers a dialogue between the Creator who becomes a creature and us created human beings, so that we might become identified with him. We relive the Gospel so that Jesus's story in Bethlehem, Nazareth, and Galilee becomes our story as we move toward Jesus's passion in Jerusalem.

7

CHRIST'S CROSS IS EVERY TREE

The Third Week

Darkness came over the whole land.

—Luke 23:44

If the ecological dimensions of the Second Week are centered on God's "cosmic plan" and Jesus, Our Creator and Lord, who becomes a creature living in the natural world that is "charged with the grandeur of God,"[1] the Third Week invites us to immerse ourselves in the world of suffering and death, which hold both humanity and the earth hostage. We are invited to contemplate these realities against the backdrop of the passion and crucifixion of Jesus Christ.

The Third Week opens with the contemplation of the Last Supper during which we focus our gaze on Jesus as he transforms created things—bread and wine—into his Body and Blood "given for all." The bread and wine are indeed "fruit of the earth," but they are not natural products. They have a story to tell of crops sowed and vines planted

IGNATIUS WAS GREEN

in the womb of the earth. They are warmed and cherished by the sun, and their roots soak up the life-giving energy of the rain. They speak of the ripening grain and vines that are pruned and tended, harvested and picked. Then comes the painful chapter in their story. The grain is ground, and the grapes are crushed and trodden underfoot to become bread and wine—bread that is broken and wine that is poured out for the life of the world. It is with this bread and wine in the hands of Jesus, blessed, broken, and given that Ignatius begins the Third Week of the *Exercises*.

The earth is inseparable to the Eucharist. Without the earth there are no grapes or grain, no bread or wine; no Body of Christ, no Eucharist. If the bread and wine, the tiny fragments born of the earth, can be the Body and Blood of Christ, then the eucharistic imagination invites us to widen our horizon and embrace a cosmic perspective of the Body of Christ in which the bread and wine represent all creation and the whole cosmos. They are sacred realities. St. Irenaeus speaks of this sacredness, when he writes: "[The Lord] has declared the cup, a part of creation, to be his own blood, from which he causes our blood to flow; and the bread, a part of creation, he has established as his own body."[2] Many years later, Teilhard de Chardin also experienced the cosmic significance of the Eucharist powerfully and articulated it with passion:

> Since once again, Lord...I have neither bread, nor wine, nor altar...I will make the whole earth my altar and on it will offer you all the labors and sufferings of the world...I will place on my paten, O God, the harvest to be won by this renewal of labor. Into my chalice I shall pour all the sap which is to be pressed out this day

Christ's Cross Is Every Tree

> from the earth's fruits....Over every living thing which is to spring up, to grow, to flower, to ripen during this day say again the words: This is my Body. And over every death-force which waits in readiness to corrode, to wither, to cut down, speak again your commanding words which express the supreme mystery of faith: This is my Blood.[3]

Amazingly, the Eucharist is the privileged place where God is now present to our world as part of that world. As Pope Francis explains in *Laudato si'*:

> It is in the Eucharist that all that has been created finds its greatest exaltation. Grace, which tends to manifest itself tangibly, found unsurpassable expression when God himself became man and gave himself as food for his creatures. The Lord, in the culmination of the mystery of the Incarnation, chose to reach our intimate depths through a fragment of matter. He comes not from above, but from within, he comes that we might find him in this world of ours. In the Eucharist, fullness is already achieved; it is the living center of the universe, the overflowing core of love and of inexhaustible life. Joined to the incarnate Son, present in the Eucharist, the whole cosmos gives thanks to God. Indeed the Eucharist is itself an act of cosmic love.[4]

But the self-giving of Jesus at the last Supper—that act of cosmic love—took place in the shadow of the cross on the eve of his passion. "This is my Body which is given

IGNATIUS WAS GREEN

for you"—given *not* taken. As Ignatius walks us through each of the events leading inexorably to Christ's death, his petition is: "grief, feeling and confusion because for my sins the Lord is going to his Passion."[5]

Ignatius provides several notes at the beginning of the Third Week to help the retreatant move as deeply as possible into the experience of Christ's passion and death. In the *Autograph* copy of the *Spiritual Exercises*, the fourth note is fascinating. In this original text, Ignatius wrote: "Consider what the humanity of Christ our Lord suffers." It appears, however, that Ignatius later introduced a correction, written in his own hand: "Consider what Christ Our Lord suffers in humanity."[6] This correction indicates that, as his spiritual experience developed, Ignatius became aware of the cosmic and interconnected dimension of the suffering of Christ on the cross. He moved from a limited, historical understanding of the personal to the universal and the cosmic. In the cry of Jesus from the cross, Ignatius heard the cry of the oppressed and the groan of the wounded earth, in whom Christ continues to suffer today, tomorrow, and always.

The Third Week moves on to describe, in great detail, the suffering of Christ, and in that pain, we hear the groan of the suffering earth today. The pain of Christ continues in the pain of an earth in ecological crisis, in the garbage heaps, in the pollution of cities, in the parched dry fields, and wherever the earth is violated. The Australian Catholic Social Justice Council summarizes very graphically that suffering in their own country:

> Production methods have often been harsh on the soil, especially in countries like Australia. Unsustainable crops, and unthinking farming

cultures, have left huge clay pans as their legacy. Deforestation has had a terrible effect on levels of salinity. Chemical sprays, fertilizers, and pesticides have been used with abandon. Our rivers are polluted and choked, with their banks collapsing and native fish dying out.[7]

St. Paul also speaks of the suffering of the whole of creation when he tells us that it is groaning, waiting with eager longing for its liberation (cf. Rom 8:19–23). St. Ignatius suggests that, in the face of the contemplation of this suffering, we ask for the grace of sorrow, compassion, and shame. These three basic attitudes are necessary if we wish to bring about an ecological conversion.

The Third Week goes beyond the contemplation of the reality of suffering to the contemplation of death. In the Gospel, we read that when Jesus breathed his last, the sun was eclipsed and "darkness came over the whole land" (Luke 23:44). We witness the death of Christ, and, in his death, that of all creatures. Even twenty years ago warnings were being sounded: "every three seconds per day, in a world characterized by oppression of the poor, a child dies of malnutrition; every minute our world is in ecological crisis, land the size of eleven football fields is lost forever from the rainforests, and every day, 137 species of life are driven into extinction.[8] Today, news sources declare that we are living "on borrowed time" with new global heat records, ocean surface temperatures rising, extreme flooding, and mass coral bleaching events in the Southern Hemisphere.

The Ignatian contemplations in the Third Week, based on the scriptural accounts of the crucifixion of Christ, underline the collusion and complicity of all the main players in the death of Jesus: Pontius Pilate, the Jewish political

IGNATIUS WAS GREEN

and religious leadership, and the ordinary people. We, too, need to recognize and acknowledge our complicity in the ecological extinction that threatens our planet, as a first step toward developing an ecological spirituality: a spirituality that echoes the touching insights in Joseph Plunkett's poem:

> I see his blood upon the rose
> And in the stars the glory of his eyes,
> His body gleams amid eternal snows,
> His tears fall from the skies.
>
> I see his face in every flower;
> The thunder and the singing of the birds
> Are but his voice—and carven by his power
> Rocks are his written words.
>
> All pathways by his feet are worn,
> His strong heart stirs the ever-beating sea,
> His crown of thorns is twined with every thorn,
> His cross is every tree.[9]

8

VERY EARLY WHEN THE SUN HAD RISEN[1]

The Fourth Week

Human beings, endowed with intelligence and love, and drawn by the fullness of Christ, are called to lead all creatures back to their Creator.

—Pope Francis, *Laudato si'* (83)

The Third Week of the *Exercises* draws to a close at night, in a garden shrouded in darkness, while the Fourth Week opens in the same garden caressed by the rays of the sunrise of the "first day of the week" (John 20:1). Ignatius invites us to contemplate the appearances of the risen Christ—of creation renewed—within the framework of the natural environment. What the Celtic Wayfarer—those guides who take people around Ireland—would call the "place of resurrection"[1]—where heaven bends down to kiss the earth into life—a space of deep awareness of the harmony and

---
1. See Mark 16:2.

IGNATIUS WAS GREEN

wholeness of all things. Or in the words of St. Paul, where "and through him God was pleased to reconcile to himself all things, whether on earth or in heaven" (Col 1:20).

As in the Second and Third Weeks of the *Spiritual Exercises*, in the Fourth Week, Ignatius invites us to focus our gaze on the person of Jesus Christ in the Gospels. Our prayer and contemplation, however, are now centered on the risen Christ, whose "cosmic mission" continues and who transcends time and space, reaching out to embrace everyone and everything, forever and beyond. He is now present everywhere in the universe. He is the "divine milieu,"[2] the cosmic Christ in whom we "live and move and have our being" (Acts 17:28).

Ignatius lists the apparitions of the risen Christ recounted in the Gospels and the letters of St. Paul. Several of them take place against the backdrop of the natural world; three happen in the garden, one along a long dusty road, and yet another on the shore of the Sea of Galilee with a charcoal fire and fish, lots of fish, while the setting of the final appearance is the Mount of Olives.

Ignatian contemplation encourages us to focus on the details of the scenes, allowing us to enter fully into the sanctuary of the presence of the risen Christ. It is the women who first encounter the risen Christ, the Lord of all creation, in the garden, for according to the Gospel, Jesus was buried in "a new tomb" in a garden (John 19:41). Mary Magdalene goes there as the sun is rising and tingeing the horizon with its gentle blush, chasing away the shadows and revealing the trees and shrubs. We see the tomb is empty but standing behind her in the garden, a silhouette against the dawn sky, is the figure of the risen Christ, whom she mistakes for the gardener, the person who cares for and tends the garden. As we watch and listen, it is Jesus's

Very Early When the Sun Had Risen

voice that Mary recognizes when he speaks her name; a voice resonant with consoling memories, breaking into and transforming her saddened present, and reaching out into the future, sharing the challenge of his mission: "Go and tell my brothers [and sisters]..." (Matt 28:10).

Luke tells the story of the appearance of Jesus who joins two disciples as they are walking along the road, a country lane from Jerusalem to Emmaus. The distance was approximately seven miles, and the journey would have taken them about three hours. Having set out in the heat of the afternoon, it was in the evening, as the shadows began to lengthen in the setting sun, that Jesus caught up with them on their way. There was a chill in the air and the dusty path was hard. They were surrounded by the country smells, the crickets, and maybe even the darting fireflies. Amid this evening stillness, heavy with the disciples' grief and disappointment yet vibrant and humming with life, we contemplate the risen Christ, "the firstborn of all creation...the firstborn from the dead" (Col 1:15, 18).

Jesus and the disciples come to the village, and because "it is almost evening and the day is now nearly over" (Luke 24:29), they go into the disciples' house and sit down at a table to eat. There, the risen Jesus breaks bread, a eucharistic gesture that embraces the past, present, and future, lighting up the darkness in the eyes of the disciples and caressing their hearts with excitement and joy. Jesus takes bread. The story of bread already speaks of the natural world, seeds and soil, rain and sunshine, but, in this eucharistic/resurrection context of the Fourth Week of the *Exercises*, the symbolism takes on a new dynamic meaning: bread blessed from now on and forever is pregnant with God.

Jesus also appears waiting on the shore of the gently lapping Sea of Galilee. The disciples had toiled all night,

IGNATIUS WAS GREEN

fishing in the water without a single catch. Again, with the sun rising above the sea, sparkling on the waves, the risen Christ is watching them from the beach. He invites them to try once more and their net fills to overflowing with wriggling, flapping silver fish—the Gospel adds, with a flourishing touch, that they were all "large fish, a hundred fifty-three of them" (John 21:11). In this littoral environment, Jesus shares his pastoral, cosmic ministry with his followers.

Finally, Jesus and his disciples climb the Mount of Olives, named after the olive trees covering its slopes. There "when he had said this, as they were watching, he was lifted up, and a cloud took him out of their sight" (Acts 1:9). As Pope Francis notes, "With the Ascension, something new and beautiful happened: Jesus brought our humanity, our flesh, into heaven — this is the first time—that is, he brought it in God. That humanity that he had assumed on earth did not remain here. The risen Jesus was not a spirit, no. He had his human body, flesh and bones, everything. He will be there in God forever."[3]

Of course, Ignatius invites retreatants to pray with all the Gospel accounts of the appearances of the risen Christ, not only the ones that take place in a natural environment. But in so doing, he incorporates into the Fourth Week an invitation to engage and interact with the risen Christ, the Lord of heaven and earth, in his totality. Jesus of Nazareth is no longer the focus of our attention. Now, it is the transformed, cosmic Christ and his global mission, lifted out of time into eternity, that fills our hearts and minds.

Ignatius anticipates the contemplations of the appearance of the risen Christ with an important "consideration": "Consider how the Divinity, which seemed to hide Itself in the Passion, now appears and shows Itself so marvelously

Very Early When the Sun Had Risen

in the most holy Resurrection by Its true and most holy effects."[4] Pope Francis describes those effects powerfully in *Laudato si'*:

> The ultimate destiny of the universe is in the fullness of God, which has already been attained by the risen Christ, the measure of the maturity of all things....The ultimate purpose of other creatures is not to be found in us. Rather, all creatures are moving forward with us and through us towards a common point of arrival, which is God, in that transcendent fullness where the risen Christ embraces and illumines all things. Human beings, endowed with intelligence and love, and drawn by the fullness of Christ, are called to lead all creatures back to their Creator.[5]

And later, Pope Francis notes, "Jesus says, 'I make all things new.' Eternal life will be a shared experience of awe, in which each creature, resplendently transfigured, will take its rightful place."[6]

At the end of each contemplation of the appearances of the risen Christ, Ignatius proposes the usual colloquy, "according to the subject matter."[7] Did the circumstances suggest to Ignatius a conversation with the Trinity: God the Father, God the Son, and God the Holy Spirit? In the Second Week, Ignatius invited us to watch and listen to the involvement of the Trinity in the incarnation, when God visited creation as a creature, as a man. And just as the whole Trinity was united in making that happen, the Trinity was also intimately involved in the resurrection. St. Peter announces to his readers that God the Father raised Jesus from the dead: "You killed the Author of life,

IGNATIUS WAS GREEN

whom God raised from the dead" (Acts 3:15). While John reports Jesus's words: "For this reason the Father loves me, because I lay down my life in order to take it up again. No one takes it from me, but I lay it down of my own accord. I have power to lay it down, and I have power to take it up again" (John 10:17–18).

The risen Christ is the Son who, through his universal Lordship, illumines all things, imbuing them with his radiant presence. While the Spirit's involvement is attested in the Letter to the Romans, where Paul writes that Jesus "was declared to be Son of God with power according to the spirit of holiness by resurrection from the dead" (Rom 1:4).

In the Fourth Week of the *Spiritual Exercises*, we hear echoes of the cosmic liturgy foreseen by St. Paul whereby "the whole creation has been groaning in labor pains until now" (Rom 8:22), waiting with eager longing to be transformed, when Christ becomes "the firstborn of all creation" (Col 1:15), and everything "may be filled with all the fullness of God" (Eph 3:19). Teilhard de Chardin, who would have prayed this Week of the *Exercises* many times in his Jesuit life, referred to the earth as his altar on which he would celebrate what he called "The Mass on the World." Teilhard's great vision was a cosmic liturgy where the cosmos becomes a living host, and the Eucharist a sacrament of the earth.

9

LOVE SHOWERED ON ALL CREATION

Contemplation to Gain Love

God's love is like the sun's rays or a bubbling fountain.
—*Spiritual Exercises* (237)

The final contemplation of the *Spiritual Exercises*, Contemplation to Gain Love, is both deeply ecological and profoundly intimate. Rooted in Ignatius's ecological conversion on the banks of the Cardoner, it unlocks the key to finding God in all things. Undoubtedly the "greenest" pages of the whole text, it tenderly gathers and brings to an awe-filled closure the total ecological experience of the *Exercises*, while introducing a new way of being in the world and relating to creation.

At the same time, the Contemplation is meant to be read and prayed with deep affection, like two people in love—as in loving and being loved—heart speaking to heart. The retreatant is held lovingly in the divine embrace and in a mutual intimacy in which God's love floods one's whole being. Caressed by God's tenderness throughout the *Exercises*, we now look back at this whole process and discover, deep within, such "great good received,"[1]—all God's gifts, grace, action, tender surprises that, as Ignatius says, descend from above, filling every moment of every day with light, love, music, and song. The spontaneous and only possible response is to be completely receptive to God and totally available "that being entirely grateful, I may be able in all to love and serve His Divine Majesty."[2]

A careful unpacking of the text of the closing Contemplation reveals a return to the threefold relationship that exists among God, human beings, and all other created things. This last Contemplation is the climax toward which the whole spiritual movement, embedded in the *Exercises* has been leading us. In a spiral movement that doubles back to the Principle and Foundation and moves beyond the humbled amazement of sinful humanity of the First Week, the Contemplation takes the retreatant to new heights of awareness and ecological insight. Insights unsurpassed by previous spiritual writers, insights that echo Ignatius's own mystical experience in Manresa.

Ignatius was fully aware that people need to be able to visualize things tangibly—to see, touch, and feel, and not just to think or hear about them. Only then will they become a transforming, personal experience that allow us to find God in them. In the first Letter of St. John, he describes his encounter with Jesus in the same terms: "We declare to you what was from the beginning, what we have heard, what we have seen with our eyes, what we have looked at and touched with our hands, concerning the word of life" (1 John 1:1). We need to hold things not just in our minds but, through our senses, also in our imaginations and in our hearts. Hence, the Contemplation to Gain Love offers a journey through our lives, hand in hand with God, conversing, reminiscing together, reliving and lingering gratefully and lovingly over God's gifts to us—totally overwhelmed by amazement at how very much God loves us.

Ignatius divided this Contemplation into four stages of awareness of God's passionate love showered on the retreatant and the whole of creation. First, everything, including creation, is God's gift to us. Second, God remains present in those gifts and in creation. Third, God always continues to act in and through them and, last, we experience the goodness and divinity of God in and through everything.

A detailed reflection on each of these stages enables us to appreciate the insight developed in the Thirty-Fourth General Congregation of the Society of Jesus, the "Jesuits," that Ignatian spirituality that is based on the *Spiritual Exercises* provides a foundation for ecological awareness. The General Congregation stated:

> The mysticism flowing from the experience of Ignatius directs us simultaneously towards the mystery of God and the activity of God in his creation. Both in our personal lives of faith and in our ministries, it is never a question of choosing either God *or* the world; rather it is always God *in* the world, laboring to bring it to perfection so that the world comes, finally to be fully *in* God.[3]

Ignatius prefaces the contemplation of the four "points" with an important reminder: "that love ought to be put more in deeds than in words."[4] The "points" then unpack the multiple dimensions of God's loving action, of God's tenderness, translated into ongoing care and presence in our lives.

IGNATIUS WAS GREEN

THE FIRST POINT (234)

We bring to memory the gifts or benefits received—of creation, redemption, and other gifts particular to ourselves. We ponder with deep affection how much God our Lord has done for us, and how much he has given us of what he possesses, and consequently, how he, the same Lord, desires to give us even his very self, in accordance with his divine design.[5]

The text comprises two simple sentences that are laced with amazement and gratitude. Sentences that gradually lead us to the climax, the "wow moment"—God's dream for each of us. God has created us and has loved us into being, birthing each of us as the unique and unrepeatable person that we are, with our individual identity and giftedness. God has also restored our brokenness, sewn up the torn edges of our lives, healed and saved us, while God's blown kisses constantly whisper in our hearts: "I am yours. You are mine."

All of creation, including each of us, is God's gift. Trileigh Tucker writes that "creation is God's gift to us of home and context."[6] Or as Louis Savary states, "Creation is the Original Blessing."[7] Ignatius invites us to picture ourselves against the background of the creation of the universe, surrounded by the galaxies, planets, and stars, gazing, as it were, through the James Webb Space Telescope at incredible views of the cosmos. He invites us to listen to the "hymn of the universe," moving to the rhythm of the ever dancing and interrelated organisms and delighting in the pageant of all created things that fill the earth, knowing with gratitude that all is gift.

Alexander Schmemann, the Orthodox theologian, in his classic *Life for the World* shares a similar intuition.

Love Showered on All Creation

> In the biblical story of creation man is presented, first of all as a hungry being, and the whole world as his food....In the Bible the food that man eats, the world of which he must partake in order to live, is given to him by God, and it is given as *communion with God*....All that exists is God's gift to man and it exists to make God known to man....It is divine love made food, made life for man.[8]

Schmemann concludes that the human person, therefore, is created first and foremost not as *Homo sapiens*, but rather *Homo adorans*, the priest of this cosmic sacrament, thanking and praising God for all his gifts, given out of love.

In this First Point of the Contemplation to Gain Love, we see a development in Ignatius's thinking from that expressed in the First Week of the *Exercises*. Now, it is no longer a question of admiring all created things just "because they have sustained me despite my connivance with the destructive work of de-creation....Instead, it is a matter of praising reverencing and loving the mystery of a God who makes me a loving gift of Himself in his creatures, and they in turn lead me to Him."[9]

The First Point of the Contemplation clearly has a biblical basis, as does the complete text of the *Spiritual Exercises*. Here, we hear distinct echoes of a striking passage in the Book of Job:

> But ask the animals, and they will teach you;
> the birds of the air, and they will tell you;
> ask the plants of the earth, and they will teach
>   you;
> and the fish of the sea will declare to you.

IGNATIUS WAS GREEN

> Who among all these does not know
> that the hand of the Lord has done this?
>   (12:7–9)

Such is the ecological dimension of the First Point—the reflection on God's personal gifts for each one of us. Every created thing is a blessing from Our Creator and Lord, and we, too, are created. We are a gift endowed with many blessings: our very being and existence, everything we have and are, every moment of our lives.

THE SECOND POINT (235)

The Second Point of the Contemplation to Gain Love plunges us deeper into God's awesome outpouring of tenderness by reflecting on God's cosmic presence that enables us to find God in all things:

> To [consider] how God dwells in creatures, in the elements, giving them being, in the plants vegetating, in the animals feeling in them, in men giving them to understand:[1] and so in me, giving me being, animating me, giving me sensation and making me to understand; likewise making a temple of me, being created to the likeness and image of His Divine Majesty.[10]

Ignatius invites the retreatant to explore how God the Creator is present in all creatures on the earth. God did not create everything and just walk away, leaving it to its own devices. Rather, God continues to cradle everything in his loving care, holding everything—flora, fauna, and humanity—in existence. Creation, therefore, is holy

Love Showered on All Creation

ground inhabited by God's hidden presence, while we are a temple made in the likeness of God. And God, the source of our image and likeness, is there in that sanctuary, looking back loving at us, and surprising us in the ordinary, the extraordinary, and the least expected moments, forever and always.

Ignatius himself lived close to nature. In fact, Jerome Nadal, one of St. Ignatius's early companions, claimed that Ignatius had been given the special grace "to see and contemplate in all things, actions, and conversations the presence of God."[11] He even went as far as to recount that Ignatius was able to see the Trinity in the leaf of an orange tree. In his biography of St. Ignatius, Philip Caraman, SJ, recounts that Ribadeneira, another early companion of Ignatius, reported that "we often saw how little things became an occasion for him to lift his spirit to God, and this—even the littlest things—is admirable. The sight of a plant, flower, leaf, shrub or fruit, even a small insect, would set him off in contemplation."[12]

By the end of his life, Ignatius, we are told, "would remain late beneath the stars, letting his eyes range over their shining forms, the work of God....His glance would stray from star to star, from one bright constellation to another even brighter, even more plunged into the heights of the cosmos and he was moved by the contemplation of the lines which one day the hand of God had traced in space. For the first time the firmament appeared to him as an immense act of love."[13]

As has been noted, among modern Jesuit authors, the writer who has shared Ignatius's cosmic perspective and the sense of the divine omnipresence more than any other, of course, is Teilhard de Chardin. His classic work, *The Divine Milieu*, was to show readers how to see God everywhere. For Teilhard the "divine milieu" makes all created things translucent, so that they become epiphanies of the divine.[14]

THE THIRD POINT (236)

Ignatius knew from his own experience that God was constantly at work in his own life, "teaching," guiding, and drawing him closer at every moment and in every detail of his existence. He was also aware that God is working in and through nature, through all events and in the world. Time and space are but the stage—the sacramental context—for a God who is active and works in and through everyone and all creation. And God does this for "me"—for each one of us.

Fr. Gonzalez-Buelta, SJ, also captures this experience of this point in his poem "No un Dios Solo" ("Not a God Alone"):

> God alone is sufficient
> But not a God
> For whom it is not sufficient
> To walk alone
> Through the universe.
> God comes close to us
> In every being in the cosmos.
> What is for us
> Home, food
> Task and horizon.
> Cosmic communion
> That unites us with God.
> In the life that fills us
> Through the senses.

Love Showered on All Creation

His gift and presence.
In us without measure.[15]

In this Third Point, Ignatius invites the exercitant to contemplate this God who tumbles into our world, weaving our personal history, continuing to give life to creation, and keeping all things in being:

> To consider how God works and labors for me in all things created on the face of the earth that is, behaves like one who labors—as in the heavens, elements, plants, fruits, cattle, etc., giving them being, preserving them, giving them vegetation and sensation.[16]

Here, Ignatius highlights the interconnectedness among created things, us, and God. God makes this happen for us, human beings, surrounded as we are by and very much part of the evolutionary process that populates our planet with creatures, including ourselves, interacting in life-sustaining ecosystems. Teilhard de Chardin, described it succinctly, "By means of all created things without exception the divine assails us, penetrates us, and moulds us."[17]

In her book *Ask the Beasts*, Elizabeth Johnson posits a similar thesis: "If you interrogate the fauna and flora of land, air, and, sea...the response will lead your mind and heart to the living God, generous source and sustaining power of their life."[18]

Contemplating God's loving activity in creation is the inspiration that underpins Ignatian apostolic spirituality, "Contemplation in Action." Rooted in the Contemplation to Gain Love, it echoes the Call of Christ the King in the Second Week of the *Exercises*, summoning those who wish to follow Christ and to labor with him. The invitation is to share in Christ's activity and be part of his cosmic mission. It also echoes what we noted earlier at the Jesuit Thirty-Fourth General Congregation, confirming the interpretation of the Ignatian text.[19]

> The mysticism flowing from the experience of Ignatius directs us simultaneously towards the mystery of God and the activity of God in his creation. Both in our personal lives of faith and our ministries, it is never a question of choosing either God or the world; rather, it is always God in the world, labouring to bring it to perfection so that the world comes, finally, to be fully in God.[20]

THE FOURTH POINT (237)

Finally, St. Ignatius moves from God's gifts and activity—from the "to which" and "in which"—in human beings and all created things, to the "from where" of the transcendent God, the Source of everything. Here, Ignatius envisages all gifts and blessings as poured out and lavished upon us by God the Creator from whom all things flow:

> To [consider] how all the good things and gifts descend from above, as my [limited] power from the supreme and infinite power from above; and so justice, goodness, pity, mercy, etc.; as from the sun descend the rays, from the fountain the waters, etc.[21]

This text recalls one of the visions that Ignatius recounts in his autobiography immediately before his description of

Love Showered on All Creation

his experience on the banks of the Cardoner. In that vision, he states that "God permitted him to understand how He had created this world. This vision presented to him a white object, with rays emanating from it. From this object God sent forth light."[22]

The text contains two key concepts that are critical for understanding Ignatius's thought and which capture his entire spirituality:

- "all the good things and gifts descend from above," and
- "as my limited power from the supreme and infinite power from above."

Ignatius uses two graphic images to illustrate his first idea. The sun's rays that bathe everything in light, and the waters that overflow from their source, bubbling down onto everything below. His intuition that all descends from above is critical to understanding that one can find all things in God, and God in all things, because everything comes from God, is bright and alive with God, and speaks of God. For Ignatius, we can find God by entering into creation. There, we are embraced and warmed through and through by the "rays" of God's love, while God's tender generosity washes over us and soaks into our whole being, transforming our lives.

Ignatius also suggests that we reflect on our positive qualities: our goodness, justice, and mercy; our "God-like qualities," in the knowledge that they are merely tiny reflections of God's goodness, justice, and mercy. We realize that we are bearers of tiny finite fragments of an infinite God. This is the treasure that God shares with us so that those

IGNATIUS WAS GREEN

around us "may see your good works and give glory to your Father in heaven" (Matt 5:16).

Commenting on the Contemplation to Gain Love, Hugo Rahner, SJ, opines: "From then [Manresa] on, his theological thought became a descending movement from God to creatures, in which created things and all earthly beauty, wisdom and righteousness were merely the reflected splendour of what he had already grasped in the immediacy of his mystical contemplation of God Himself."[23]

While, the Irish Jesuit theologian, Brian O'Leary, writing of the love of God in the Fourth Week of the *Exercises*, writes:

> There I encounter a God who showers his gifts and blessings on me, and who desires, as far as he can, to give himself to me; a God who dwells in all creatures, including me, indeed who makes a temple of me; a God who works and labours for me in all creatures and, we must add, in me for all creatures; a God who is the source of all human goodness and virtue, who in some sense, shares his own goodness and virtue with me.[24]

Again, the spontaneous movement arising from grateful love and from having discerned the presence of God in all created things is to ask God, Our Creator and Lord, to take our whole being for God's service and the service of others and creation.

We no longer wish "to live for ourselves alone" but for God, for our brothers and sisters, and in a new relationship with our common home. This is the ecological conversion that *The Spiritual Exercises of St. Ignatius* facilitate.

10

CONCLUSION

Green Was Ignatius's Passion

On feast days in the Catholic liturgy, the second preface to the Eucharistic Prayer begins: "You renew the Church in every age by raising up men and women outstanding in holiness, living witnesses of Your unchanging love."[1] St. Ignatius of Loyola lived when most people viewed reality through the anthropocentric lens of the Renaissance, and hence, needed a new way to find God in all things—to discover a cosmic spirituality. Today, we live in a broken and wounded world, enmeshed in a violent and predatory culture that appears to be deliberately snapping twigs off the tree of life. Ignatius had peered into the sky from his early life in Loyola until his final years when he sat in Rome and gazed at the night sky glittering with stars. He had felt the breath of creation and saw life and the whole universe as God's gift calling forth wonder and gratitude in our hearts. We live far in thought and sensitivity from St. Ignatius's sixteenth-century context, but we now need Ignatius's vision more than ever. As we have seen, the text of the *Spiritual Exercises* contains many insights that nurture a sorely needed ecological spirituality for the twenty-first century.

IGNATIUS WAS GREEN

Ignatius avoided the anthropocentric approach, focused on the human race that was so common in his day, and in ours, too. Instead, he introduces us as essentially relational creatures. His God-centered text imparts a passion for the Creator and for creation. From the very beginning of the *Exercises*, Ignatius refers to God as our Creator and Lord. In the Principle and Foundation, creation is a sacred space that speaks to us of God and leads us to God. In that space, possession is transformed into stewardship, dominion changes into collaboration, and exploitation becomes a respectful use of other creatures. Hence, creation is not a commodity to be used and abused. According to the Jesuits, that abuse happens because a "lack of respect for a loving Creator leads to a denial of the dignity of the human person and the wanton destruction of the environment."[2]

The First Week of the *Exercises* focuses on sin and the sinner, tenderly loved by God, and embraced by creation, despite our chapter in the story of the human roots of the environmental crisis. It helps us to acknowledge our complicity in that crisis and to "taste, sense, feel sin"[3] in all its horror. Acceptance of our collusion is the first step in the process of reconciliation and conversion. "We might," the Jesuits suggest, "do something to protect the environment or promote ecology, if we sincerely repent our sins of complicity, if we learn to recognize and acknowledge them in the spirit of the First Week of the Exercises."[4]

Ignatius offers a powerful motivation in our commitment to act for the sake of the earth, in the Second Week of the *Exercises*, by exposing us to the irresistible attraction of Jesus of Nazareth and his invitation to join him in the re-creation of a new heaven and a new earth, his cosmic mission. This is no human endeavor. The call is not to

Conclusion

dominate the earth but to renew it; ecological commitment is a form of discipleship, of following Jesus.

The meditations on the incarnation and the nativity that follow invite us to contemplate how God, in Jesus, unites divinity and humanity—the Creator with creation. There, we meet the created world as the place to encounter and converse with God made human, who steps into time and space. Jesus is born in a specific place, Nazareth, where he walks our earth, breathes our air, and lives our life. He shares with us a deep relationship with creation, enabling us to be in communion with the created order.

Ignatius raises our ecological consciousness in the Third Week of the *Exercises* by inviting us to contemplate the effects of pain, suffering, and death in humanity and creation. Awareness must precede action. This consciousness opens the door to the climax of the *Exercises* where we discover and are drawn into communion with our risen Redeemer and with the whole of renewed creation. We find ourselves in a new place, at the center of the universe, in the heart of love. God has laid, and is laying, the foundation of what we can accomplish. So, we too can touch the earth with tenderness.

The final contemplation of the Fourth Week of the *Exercises* is really a narrative of God's evolutionary relationship with the world, a relationship in which we are invited to share. It goes far to correcting our diminished understanding of God's presence and continual activity in creation. Ignatius helps us to grasp that caring for the earth is an intrinsic part of our love for God and is what makes us most Godlike. In the words of Caitlin Matthews: "On the path to going home, you will remember that you are part of everything. When you look after the Earth, when you defend the helpless, when you speak for those that have no

IGNATIUS WAS GREEN

voice, when you enjoy and respect my creation, then you will be most like me."[5]

Above all, in the *Spiritual Exercises*, Ignatius articulates the conviction that underpins ecological spirituality: the interconnectedness of all things, the radical interdependence of all creatures. He affirms that God, humanity, and the world are interlinked. For Ignatius, spirituality was not just about God and us, and nothing else. Rather, he recognized the value and the goodness of nonhuman creation. The Jesuits' Decree, "Our Mission and Culture," reminds us that

> Ignatius proclaims that for human beings there is no authentic search for God without an insertion into the life of the creation, and that, on the other hand, all solidarity with human beings and every engagement with the created world cannot be authentic without a discovery of God.[6]

The Spiritual Exercises of St. Ignatius of Loyola were born at a different time and in a different place, but they are most definitely "green." They offer both *radical reflection* and a *call to action* as an alternative to the dominant materialistic and reductionist approach that is largely disconnected from ecological concerns today.

Ignatian spirituality overflows with ecological insights that speak to those concerns. The whimper of our wounded earth surely finds an echo in his passionate Basque heart. Yes, Ignatius was definitely *green*. It is who he always was—his identity—that has been beautifully captured by Cameron Bellm:

Conclusion

Before the vigil at Montserrat,
Before the pilgrimage to Jerusalem,
Before the foundation of the Society,
There was a man, on a castle balcony,
Gazing up in wonder at the stars.
St. Ignatius, awed by mystery,
Draw our eyes ever upward to the heavens,
Our hearts to the holy adventures that await us,
And our spirits to the grandeur that surrounds us.
May we, too, see all things within us and beyond us
As sacred galaxies, formed and held,
This year and always, by loving hands.
Amen.[7]

Notes

INTRODUCTION

1. See: https://www.gipuzkoaturismoa.eus/en/things-to-do/scenery-and-nature.
2. Joseph N. Tylenda, SJ, *A Pilgrim's Journey. The Autobiography of Ignatius of Loyola* (San Francisco: Ignatius Press, 2001), 7.
3. Paul Halsall, ed., *Medieval Source Book:* "Golden Legend: St. Francis," vol. 5 (New York: Fordham University Center for Medieval Studies, 1996), https://sourcebooks.fordham.edu/basis/goldenlegend/gl-vol5-francis.asp.
4. *Medieval Source Book:* "Golden Legend: St. Francis," vol. 5.
5. Tylenda, *A Pilgrim's Journey*, 27.
6. Tylenda, *A Pilgrim's Journey*, 29.
7. Tylenda, *A Pilgrim's Journey*, 30.
8. Tylenda, *A Pilgrim's Journey*, 30.
9. In the spirit of St. Francis, Jorge Bergoglio, SJ, better known as Pope Francis, is engaged, among other things, in repairing God's Church, embracing the poor, and calling for an ecological conversion.

CHAPTER 1

1. Ellen Bernstein, "Love and compassion: How women can address the climate crisis," Earthbeat, A Project of *National Catholic Reporter*, September 20, 2023, https://www.ncronline

.org/earthbeat/viewpoints/love-and-compassion-how-women-can-address-climate-crisis.

2. Sandra M. Schneiders, "Approaches to the Study of Christian Spirituality," in *The Blackwell Companion to Christian Spirituality*, ed. Arthur Holder (Oxford: Blackwell Publishing, 2005), 16.

3. Schneiders, "Approaches to the Study of Christian Spirituality," 17.

4. Description of the Trinity attributed to St Augustine of Hippo.

5. Quote from Gerard Manley Hopkins, "As Kingfishers catch fire," 1877, https://poets.org/poem/kingfishers-catch-fire-dragonflies-draw-flame#:~:text=%C3%8D%20say%20m%C3%B3re%3A%20the%20just,is%20in%20the%20public%20domain.

6. Pope Francis, Encyclical Letter *Laudato si'*, "On Care for our Common Home," May 24, 2015, no. 84.

7. News flashes found on social media in a twenty-four-hour period in May 2023.

8. See Brian Roewe, "Citigroup shareholder support holds steady for Catholic sisters' resolution on climate, Indigenous rights," Earthbeat, A Project of *National Catholic Reporter*, April 26, 2023, https://www.ncronline.org/earthbeat/justice/citigroup-shareholder-support-holds-steady-catholic-sisters-resolution-climate.

9. Gaël Giraud, SJ, and Carlo Petrini, *The Taste for Change: Ecological Transition as the Path to Happiness* (*Il Gusto di Cambiare*) (Vatican City: Libreria Editrice Vaticana, 2023).

10. Cindy Wooden, "Join the young in fighting for the poor and the planet, pope says," Catholic News Service, May 18, 2023, https://www.usccb.org/news/2023/join-young-fighting-poor-and-planet-pope-says.

11. Pope Francis, *Laudato si'*, no. 64.

12. This does also not mean that other popes (and other parts of the Church) have not spoken about the crisis—Francis highlights the teachings of his predecessors, particularly St. John Paul II and Pope Benedict XVI.

Notes

13. Pope Francis, *Laudate Deum,* "Praise God," October 4, 2023, nos. 53, 58.

14. Cf. also Pss 19, 139.

15. Cf. James C. Ungureanu, "Retrieving an Ancient Sacramental Ecology, Part 1," *Credo,* May 28, 2021, https://credomag.com/2021/05/retrieving-an-ancient-sacramental-ecology-part-1/.

16. St. Augustine of Hippo, Sermon 68:5.

17. *Viriditas,* usually translated as "greenness" or "greening power," appears several times in the writings of Gregory the Great and Augustine. Hildegard, however, uses the term in a unique and personal way to describe the complex relationship among the Christian, creation, and God.

18. Hildegard of Bingen, *Holistic Healing* (Collegeville, MN: Liturgical Press, 1994). Original Latin title: *Causae et curae*.

19. See Gabriele Uhlheim, ed., *Meditations with Hildegard of Bingen* (Rochester, VT: Bear & Company, 1983), 35.

20. These works include: *The Pilgrim's Story,* a brief autobiographical narrative, the *Constitutions of the Society of Jesus,* personal records concerning the founding of the Society of Jesus, and more than 7,000 letters.

21. See Arturo Sosa, SJ, "Walking with Ignatius," video, Episode 9, May 3, 2022, Jesuits in Ireland, https://jesuit.ie/videos/growing-in-awareness-of-our-common-home/.

22. Douglas Burton-Christie, "Nature," in Holder, *Blackwell Companion to Christian Spirituality,* 478–92.

23. Thomas Merton, *New Seeds of Contemplation* (New York: New Directions, 2007), 30–31.

24. Thomas Berry, "The World of Wonder," in *Spiritual Ecology: The Cry of the Earth,* ed. Llewellyn Vaughan-Lee (Point Reyes, CA: The Golden Sufi Center, 2016), 23.

25. See Damian Costello, "Look to Indigenous peoples to revive true biblical ecology," *U.S. Catholic,* July 1, 2021, https://uscatholic.org/articles/202107/look-to-indigenous-peoples-to-revive-true-biblical-ecology/.

26. Ignatius often refers to God as "Our Creator and Lord" throughout the text of the *Exercises*.

IGNATIUS WAS GREEN

27. *Ignacio de Loyola. Ejercicios Espirituales. Introducción, texto notas y vocabulario*, Candido De Dalmases, S.I. (Sal Terrae, Santander, 1987; translation by author).

CHAPTER 2

1. Biographical information taken from George Ashenbrenner, *Stretched for Greater Glory* (Chicago: Loyola Press, 2004), 1–3, and Joseph Tetlow, *The Spiritual Exercises of St Ignatius Loyola* (New York: The Crossroad Publishing Company, 1992), 12–13.

2. Ignatius was baptised *Eneco* in honor of the eleventh-century abbot of the Benedictine monastery of Oña. Ignatius also attributed his recovery after his wound at Pamplona to St. Peter, for whom he had special devotion, and on the eve of whose feast day, Ignatius's fever finally broke.

3. Margaret Silf, *Just Call Me Inigo* (Chicago: Loyola Press, 2012), 6.

4. St. Ignatius of Loyola, *The Autobiography of Ignatius of Loyola*, trans. J. F. X. O'Conor (New York: Benziger Brothers, 1900), 19.

5. St. Ignatius of Loyola, *The Autobiography*, 24.

6. St. Ignatius of Loyola, *The Autobiography*, 11.

7. St. Ignatius of Loyola, *The Autobiography*, 53.

8. St. Ignatius of Loyola, *The Autobiography*, 57.

9. See Brian O'Leary, SJ, *God Ever Greater: Exploring Ignatian Spirituality* (Collegeville, MN: Liturgical Press, 2020), 64.

10. Arturo Sosa, SJ, *Walking with Ignatius: In Conversation with Dario Menor* (Dublin: Messenger Publications, 2021), 13.

11. Joseph N. Tylenda, SJ, *A Pilgrim's Journey: The Autobiography of St. Ignatius of Loyola* (San Francisco: Ignatius Press, 2001), 11.

12. Giorgio Papasogli, *Saint Ignatius of Loyola*, trans. Paul Garvin (New York: Society of St. Paul, 1957), cited in "Saint Ignatius in nature's embrace: A 3-D view, Retrospective-Perspective-

Notes

Reflective," *Ecojesuit*, May 31, 2013, https://www.ecojesuit.com/saint-ignatius-in-natures-embrace-a-3-d-view-retrospective-perspective-reflective/.

13. Philip Caraman, SJ, *Ignatius Loyola: A Biography of the Founder of the Jesuits* (San Francisco: Harper & Row, 1990), 59, cited in "Saint Ignatius in nature's embrace."

14. Fr. Christoph Genelli, *The Life of St. Ignatius of Loyola* (London: Burns, Oates, and Co., 1871), 189.

CHAPTER 3

1. The "official texts" are the *Autograph* in Spanish, so called because Ignatius corrected it in his own hand, and the Latin Vulgate of 1548, approved by Pope Paul III, and the two editions (1541 and 1547) of the Latin *versio prima*.

2. Ignatius's legs had to be rebroken to heal properly, and subsequently realizing one leg was shorter with an ugly protrusion in it, he demanded that it be rebroken and sawed down.

3. Louis J. Puhl, SJ, *The Spiritual Exercises of St. Ignatius: Based on Studies in the Language of the Autograph* (Chicago: Loyola University Press, 1951), 114–16.

4. Tylenda, *A Pilgrim's Journey*, 11.

5. Puhl, *The Spiritual Exercises of St. Ignatius*, 95.

6. Puhl, *The Spiritual Exercises of St. Ignatius*, 97.

7. Many years later, the British patriotic anthem "I Vow to Thee my Country" would echo Ignatius's experience of lifting his loyal gaze from an earthy monarch to the king of heaven.

8. St. Ignatius of Loyola, *Autobiography*, 26.

9. Above the altar, on one of the great beams is an inscription, both in Basque and Spanish, reading: *AQVI SE ENTREGÓ A DIOS INIGO DE LOYOLA* ("Here, Ignatius of Loyola surrendered to God").

10. Pope Francis, *Laudato si'*, no. 84.

11. St. Ignatius of Loyola, *Autobiography*, 18.

12. The earliest manuscripts of the *Spiritual Exercises* that we have are the "Text of John Helyar" (H), dating from 1535 to 1536, and the "Cologne Text" (C), dating from 1538 to 1539.

13. St. Ignatius of Loyola, *Autobiography*, 57.

14. St. Ignatius of Loyola, *Autobiography*, 57.

15. *Compedio Breve del Ejercitatorio de la via espiritual* (*Brief Compendium of the Book of Exercises for the Spiritual Life*) was written by the Benedictine Garcia Jimenez de Cisneros (d. 1510).

16. See Santiago Arzubialde, SJ, and Jose Garcia de Castro, SJ, eds., *The Autograph Copy of the Spiritual Exercises* (Loyola: Ediciones Mensajero, 2022), 42.

17. Puhl, *The Spiritual Exercises of St. Ignatius*, 100.

18. Louis M. Savary, *The New Spiritual Exercises: In the Spirit of Teilhard de Chardin* (Mahwah, NJ: Paulist Press, 2010), xi.

19. Puhl, *The Spiritual Exercises of St. Ignatius*, 236.

20. Peter-Hans Kolvenbach, "Our Responsibility for God's Creation," address at the opening of Arrupe College, Jesuit School of Philosophy and Humanities, Harare, Zimbabwe, August 22, 1998 (Ottawa: The Jesuits Centre for Social Faith and Justice, 1999), 12.

21. Puhl, *The Spiritual Exercises of St. Ignatius*, 15.

22. Puhl, *The Spiritual Exercises of St. Ignatius*, 230–37.

23. Puhl, *The Spiritual Exercises of St. Ignatius*, 316.

CHAPTER 4

1. In Ignatius's words, the *Exercises* are intended "to overcome oneself and to order one's life, without reaching a decision through some disordered affection," 21.

2. See Eric Jensen, SJ, *The Spiritual Exercises of Saint Ignatius Loyola, with Translations in English* (Guelph Canada: Ignatius Jesuit Center), 5.

3. Jensen, *The Spiritual Exercises*, 1.

4. Jensen, *The Spiritual Exercises*, 15.

Notes

5. Pierre Teilhard de Chardin, "Mass on the World," in *The Heart of Matter* (San Francisco: HarperOne, 2002), 131–32.
6. Jensen, *The Spiritual Exercises*, 23.
7. Jensen, *The Spiritual Exercises*, 23.
8. See Gerard Manley Hopkins, "God's Grandeur," https://www.poetryfoundation.org/poems/44395/gods-grandeur.
9. Gerald M. Fagin, SJ, *Putting on the Heart of Christ: How the Spiritual Exercises Invite Us to a Virtuous Life* (Chicago: Loyola Press, 2010), 25.
10. See John Reilly, SJ, "Principle and Foundation: A Contemporary Version," May 6, 2011, https://orientations.jesuits.ca/pandf_reilly.html.
11. Savary, *The New Spiritual Exercises*, 47.
12. Caitlin Matthews, *The Blessing Seed: A Creation Myth for the New Millennium* (Bath: Barefoot Books, 1998), 1–6, 9–10.

CHAPTER 5

1. Martin Luther King Jr., "Man's Sin and God's Grace," sermon in Montgomery, 1960, https://kinginstitute.stanford.edu/king-papers/documents/mans-sin-and-gods-grace.
2. For a more detailed consideration of this topic cf. James Profit, SJ, "Spiritual Exercises and Ecology," *Promotio Iustitiae* 82 (2004): 6–11.
3. Pope Francis, "Show Mercy to Our Common Home," pope's message for the World Day of Prayer for the Care of Creation, September 1, 2016, https://press.vatican.va/content/salastampa/en/bollettino/pubblico/2016/09/01/160901b.html.
4. "'We Live in a Broken World'—Reflections on Ecology," *Promotio Iustitiae* 70 (1999), Social Apostolate Secretariat at the General Curia of the Jesuits, Rome, http://www.sjweb.info/sjs/documents/pj_070_eng.pdf.
5. Jensen, *The Spiritual Exercises*, 50.
6. Jensen, *The Spiritual Exercises*, 58.

7. Jensen, *The Spiritual Exercises*, 56.
8. Jensen, *The Spiritual Exercises*, 60.
9. Cf. Pope Francis, *Laudato si'*, no. 1.
10. Jensen, *The Spiritual Exercises*, 61.
11. Matthews, *The Blessing Seed*, 22.
12. Jensen, *The Spiritual Exercises*, 53.
13. Pope Francis, *Laudato si'*, no. 217.

CHAPTER 6

1. In the original Spanish text, Ignatius titles this meditation: *El llamamiento del Rey temporal ayuda a contemplar la vida del Rey Eternal* ("The Call of the Temporal King. It helps to contemplate the life of the King Eternal").
2. Jensen, *The Spiritual Exercises*, 95.
3. Jensen, *The Spiritual Exercises*, 97.
4. Jensen, *The Spiritual Exercises*, 98.
5. Savary, *The New Spiritual Exercises*, 79.
6. Savary, *The New Spiritual Exercises*, 77.
7. Jensen, *The Spiritual Exercises*, 102.
8. David L. Fleming, SJ, *Draw Me Into Your Friendship: The Spiritual Exercises; A Literal Translation and a Contemporary Reading* (St. Louis: Institute of Jesuit Sources, 1996), 90.
9. Fleming, *Draw Me into Your Friendship*, 91.
10. Jensen, *The Spiritual Exercises*, 104.

CHAPTER 7

1. Gerard Manley Hopkins, "God's Grandeur."
2. St. Irenaeus, *Against Heresies* 5:2. http://ww1.antiochian.org/church-fathers-holy-eucharist#:~:text=%22He%20has%20declared%20the%20cup,gives%20increase%20unto%20our%20bodies.

Notes

3. Teilhard de Chardin, *The Heart of the Matter* (San Francisco: HarperOne, 2002), 118–19.

4. Pope Francis, *Laudato si'*, no. 236.

5. Jensen, *The Spiritual Exercises*, 193.

6. Jensen, *The Spiritual Exercises*, 195.

7. Gerard Moore, SM, *Eucharist and Justice*, Catholic Social Justice Series (Sydney: Australian Catholic Justice Council, 2000), 17–18.

8. Today, news sources declare that we are living "on borrowed time" with new global heat records, ocean surface temperatures rising, extreme flooding, and mass coral bleaching events in the Southern Hemisphere. See "'On borrowed time': World marks new global heat record in March," Aljazeera.com, Thursday, April 9, 2024, https://www.aljazeera.com/news/2024/4/9/on-borrowed-time-world-marks-new-global-heat-record-in-march.

9. Joseph Mary Plunkett, "I See His Blood upon the Rose," http://poetry.elcore.net/CatholicPoets/Plunkett/Plunkett29.html.

CHAPTER 8

1. For the Celtic saints, the place of resurrection was the place God was calling you to, the place where you would worship, work, and pray until Christ comes to take you home.

2. Savary, *The New Spiritual Exercises*, 167.

3. Pope Francis, *Regina Caeli*, Feast of the Ascension, Saint Peter's Square, May 21, 2023, https://www.vatican.va/content/francesco/en/angelus/2023/documents/20230521-regina-caeli.html.

4. Jensen, *The Spiritual Exercises*, 223.

5. Pope Francis, *Laudato si'*, no. 83.

6. Pope Francis, *Laudato si'*, no. 243.

7. Jensen, *The Spiritual Exercises*, 225.

IGNATIUS WAS GREEN

CHAPTER 9

1. Jensen, *The Spiritual Exercises*, 233.
2. Jensen, *The Spiritual Exercises*, 233.
3. Society of Jesus, "Our Mission and Culture," *General Congregation* 34 (1995), no. 7, https://jesuitportal.bc.edu/research/documents/1995_decree4gc34/.
4. Jensen, *The Spiritual Exercises*, 230.
5. See Jensen, *The Spiritual Exercises*, 234.
6. Trileigh Tucker, "Ecology and the Spiritual Exercises," *The Way* 43, no. 1 (2004): 7.
7. Savary, *The New Spiritual Exercises*, 178.
8. Alexander Schmemann, *Life for the World: Sacraments and Orthodoxy* (New York: St. Vladimir Seminary Press, 2000), 14.
9. Society of Jesus, "'We Live in a Broken World'—Reflections on Ecology," *Promotio Iustitiae* 70 (April 1999).
10. Jensen, *The Spiritual Exercises*, 235.
11. See Avery Dulles, "Ignatius among Us: Great 20th-century theologians share a common spiritual heritage," *America*, February 4, 2013, https://www.americamagazine.org/issue/vantage-point/ignatius-among-us.
12. See Philip Caraman, SJ, *Ignatius Loyola: A Biography of the Founder of the Jesuits* (San Francisco: Harper and Row, 1990), 59; see also Hedwig Lewis, SJ, "Saint Ignatius in nature's embrace," *Ecojesuit*, May 31, 2013.
13. Giorgio Papasogli, *Saint Ignatius of Loyola*, trans. Paul Garvin (New York: Society of St Paul, 1957), cited in Lewis, "Saint Ignatius in nature's embrace."
14. Pierre Teilhard de Chardin, *The Divine Milieu* (New York: Harper and Row, 1968).
15. Benjamín González Buelta, SJ, *No un Dios Solo* ("Not a God Alone") in *Psalms to Accompany the Spiritual Exercises of St. Ignatius of Loyola*, trans. Damian Howard (Hants, UK: Way Publications, 2012), https://www.theway.org.uk/. Used with permission.
16. Jensen, *The Spiritual Exercises*, 236.

Notes

17. Teilhard de Chardin, *The Divine Milieu*, 112.

18. Elizabeth Johnson, *Ask the Beasts: Darwin and the God of Love* (New York: Bloomsbury Continuum, 2015), 2.

19. Society of Jesus, "Our Mission and Culture," *General Congregation* 34 (1995), no. 7.

20. Society of Jesus, *General Congregation* 34, D4, 7.

21. Jensen, *The Spiritual Exercises*, 237.

22. St. Ignatius of Loyola, *Autobiography of St. Ignatius*, 55.

23. Hugo Rahner, *Ignatius the Theologian*, trans. Michael Barry (New York: Herder and Herder, 1986), 4, cited by Howard Gray, SJ, "The Experience of Ignatius Loyola: Background to Jesuit Education," address delivered at Fordham University, October 15, 1999.

24. Brian O'Leary, SJ, "The Mysticism of Ignatius Loyola," *Review for Ignatian Spirituality* 116, no. 6 (2007): 79.

CONCLUSION

1. United States Conference of Catholic Bishops, "Preface II," *Roman Missal* (Collegeville, MN: Liturgical Press, 2011), 600.

2. Under "Challenging Context," GC33, D.1, n. 35, cited in Society of Jesus, "We Live in a Broken World," *Promotio Iustitiae* 70, 1999, http://www.sjweb.info/sjs/documents/pj_070_eng.pdf.

3. Jensen, *The Spiritual Exercises*, 48–52.

4. Society of Jesus, "We Live in a Broken World," 2.2.

5. Matthews, *The Blessing Seed*, 24.

6. Society of Jesus, "Decree 4: 'Our Mission and Culture,'" GC34 (1995), no. 86, https://jesuits-eum.org/gc-decrees/our-mission-and-culture/.

7. Cameron Bellm, "Ignatius and the Stars: A Prayer for the Close of the Ignatian Year," Available at: Jesuits.org and used as part of the Spirit & Verse series sponsored by the Jesuit Conference of Canada and the United States.

Selected Bibliography

PRIMARY SOURCES

Golden Legend, The, or *Lives of the Saints*. Compiled by Jacobus de Voragine, Archbishop of Genoa, 1275. First edition published 1470. Translated by William Caxton, first edition 1483. Edited by F. S. Ellis, Temple Classics, 1900, vol. 5. This text is part of the *Internet Medieval Source Book*, edited by Paul Halsall. New York: Fordham University Center for Medieval Studies, 1996. https://sourcebooks.fordham.edu/basis/goldenlegend/gl-vol5-francis.asp.

Hildegard of Bingen. *Holistic Healing*. Collegeville, MN: Liturgical Press, 1994.

St. Ignatius Loyola. *The Autobiography of Ignatius of Loyola*. Translated by J. F. X. O'Conor. New York: Benziger Brothers, 1900.

Jensen, Eric, SJ. *The Spiritual Exercises of Saint Ignatius Loyola, with Translations in English*. Guelph Canada: Ignatius Jesuit Center.

PAPAL DOCUMENTS

Pope Francis. Apostolic Exhortation *Laudate Deum*. "Praise God." October 4, 2023.

———. Encyclical Letter *Laudato si'*. "On Care for Our Common Home." May 24, 2015.

———. *Regina Caeli*. Feast of the Ascension. Saint Peter's Square, May 21, 2023. https://www.vatican.va/content/francesco/en/angelus/2023/documents/20230521-regina-caeli.html.

IGNATIUS WAS GREEN

———. "Show Mercy to our Common Home." Pope's message for the World Day of Prayer for the Care of Creation, September 1, 2016. https://press.vatican.va/content/salastampa/en/bollettino/pubblico/2016/09/01/160901b.html.

OTHER BOOKS

Arzubialde, SJ, Santiago, and Jose Garcia de Castro, SJ, eds. *The Autograph Copy of the Spiritual Exercises*. Loyola: Ediciones Mensajero, 2022.

Ashenbrenner, George. *Stretched for Greater Glory*. Chicago: Loyola Press, 2004.

Berry, Thomas. "The World of Wonder." In *Spiritual Ecology: The Cry of the Earth*, edited by Llewellyn Vaughan-Lee, 21–30. Point Reyes, CA: The Golden Sufi Center, 2016.

Burton-Christie, Douglas. "Nature." In *The Blackwell Companion to Christian Spirituality*, edited by Arthur Holder, 478–92. Oxford: Blackwell Publishing, 2005.

Caraman, SJ, Philip. *Ignatius Loyola: A Biography of the Founder of the Jesuits*. San Francisco: Harper & Row, 1990.

Fagin, SJ, Gerald M. *Putting on the Heart of Christ: How the Spiritual Exercises Invite Us to a Virtuous Life*. Chicago: Loyola Press, 2010.

Fleming, SJ, David L. *Draw Me into Your Friendship: The Spiritual Exercises; A Literal Translation and Contemporary Reading*. St. Louis: Institute of Jesuit Sources, 1996.

Genelli, Father Christoph. *The Life of St. Ignatius of Loyola*. London: Burns, Oates, and Co., 1871.

Giraud, SJ, Gaël, and Carlo Petrini. *The Taste for Change: Ecological Transition as the Path to Happiness (Il Gusto di Cambiare)*. Vatican City: Libreria Editrice Vaticana, 2023.

Johnson, Elizabeth. *Ask the Beasts: Darwin and the God of Love*. New York: Bloomsbury Continuum, 2015.

Matthews, Caitlin. *The Blessing Seed: A Creation Myth for the New Millennium*. Bath: Barefoot Books, 1998.

Selected Bibliography

Merton, Thomas. *New Seeds of Contemplation*. New York: New Directions, 2007.

Moore, SM, Gerard. *Eucharist and Justice*. Catholic Social Justice Series. Sydney: Australian Catholic Justice Council, 2000.

O'Leary, SJ, Brian. *God Ever Greater: Exploring Ignatian Spirituality*. Collegeville, MN: Liturgical Press, 2020.

Papasogli, Giorgio. *Saint Ignatius of Loyola*. Translated by Paul Garvin. New York: Society of St. Paul, 1957.

Puhl, Louis J, SJ. *The Spiritual Exercises of St. Ignatius*. Based on Studies in the Language of the Autograph. Chicago: Loyola University Press, 1951.

Rahner, Hugo. *Ignatius the Theologian*. Translated by Michael Barry. New York: Herder and Herder, 1986.

Savary, Louis M. *The New Spiritual Exercises: In the Spirit of Teilhard de Chardin*. Mahwah, NJ: Paulist Press, 2010.

Schmemann, Alexander. *Life for the World: Sacraments and Orthodoxy*. New York: St. Vladimir Seminary Press, 2000.

Schneiders, Sandra M. "Approaches to the Study of Christian Spirituality." In *The Blackwell Companion to Christian Spirituality*, edited by Arthur Holder, 15–34. Oxford: Blackwell Publishing, 2005.

Silf, Margaret. *Just Call Me Inigo*. Chicago: Loyola Press, 2012.

Sosa, SJ, Arturo. *Walking with Ignatius: In conversation with Dario Menor*. Dublin: Messenger Publications, 2021.

Teilhard de Chardin, Pierre. *The Divine Milieu*. New York, Harper and Row, 1968.

———. "Mass on the World." In *The Heart of Matter*. San Francisco: HarperOne, 2002.

Tetlow, Joseph. *The Spiritual Exercises of St Ignatius Loyola*. New York: The Crossroad Publishing Company, 1992.

Tylenda, SJ, Joseph N. *A Pilgrim's Journey: The Autobiography of Ignatius of Loyola*. San Francisco: Ignatius Press, 2001.

Uhlein Gabriele, ed. *Meditations with Hildegard of Bingen*. Rochester, VT: Bear & Company, 1983.

ARTICLES

Bernstein, Ellen. "Love and compassion: How women can address the climate crisis." Earthbeat, a Project of National Catholic Reporter, September 20, 2023. https://www.ncronline.org/earthbeat/viewpoints/love-and-compassion-how-women-can-address-climate-crisis.

Connor, Steve. "How a century of destruction has laid bare the world's rain forests." *Independent*, Saturday, July 10, 2004. https://www.independent.co.uk/climate-change/news/how-a-century-of-destruction-has-laid-bare-the-world-s-rainforests-5356170.html.

Costello, Damian. "Look to Indigenous peoples to revive true biblical ecology," *U.S. Catholic*, July 1, 2021. https://uscatholic.org/articles/202107/look-to-indigenous-peoples-to-revive-true-biblical-ecology/.

Dulles, Avery. "Ignatius among us: Great 20th-century theologians share a common spiritual heritage." *America*, February 4, 2013. https://www.americamagazine.org/issue/vantage-point/ignatius-among-us.

Gray, Howard, SJ. "The Experience of Ignatius Loyola: Background to Jesuit Education." Address delivered at Fordham University, October 15, 1999.

Kolvenbach, Peter-Hans. "Our Responsibility for God's Creation." Address at the opening of Arrupe College, Jesuit School of Philosophy and Humanities, Harare, Zimbabwe, August 22, 1998. Ottawa: The Jesuits Centre for Social Faith and Justice, 1999.

Lewis, SJ, Hedwig. "Saint Ignatius in Nature's Embrace: A 3-D view, Retrospective-Perspective-Reflective." *Ecojesuit*, May 31, 2013. https://www.ecojesuit.com/saint-ignatius-in-natures-embrace-a-3-d-view-retrospective-perspective-reflective/.

O'Leary, SJ, Brian. "The Mysticism of Ignatius Loyola." *Review for Ignatian Spirituality* 116, no. 6 (2007).

"'On borrowed time': World marks new global heat record in March." Aljazeera.com, Thursday, April 9, 2024. https://www.aljazeera

Selected Bibliography

.com/news/2024/4/9/on-borrowed-time-world-marks-new-global-heat-record-in-march.

Profit, SJ, James. "Spiritual Exercises and Ecology." *Promotio Iustitiae* 82, (2004).

Reilly, SJ, John. "Principle and Foundation: A Contemporary Version." May 6, 2011. https://orientations.jesuits.ca/pandf_reilly.html.

Society of Jesus. *General Congregation* 34 (1995). https://jesuitportal.bc.edu/research/documents/1995_decree4gc34/.

———. "'We Live in a Broken World'—Reflections on Ecology." *Promotio Iustitiae* 70 (1999), Social Apostolate Secretariat at the General Curia of the Jesuits, Rome. http://www.sjweb.info/sjs/documents/pj_070_eng.pdf.

Tucker, Trileigh. "Ecology and the Spiritual Exercises." *The Way* 43, no. 1 (2004).

Ungureanu, James C. "Retrieving an Ancient Sacramental Ecology, Part 1." *Credo*, May 28, 2021.

Wooden, Cindy. "Join the young in fighting for the poor and the planet, pope says." USCCB.org, May 18, 2023. https://www.usccb.org/news/2023/join-young-fighting-poor-and-planet-pope-says.

www.ingramcontent.com/pod-product-compliance
Lightning Source LLC
Chambersburg PA
CBHW071729090426
42738CB00011B/2428